DEEP INTO THE BITCOIN RABBIT HOLE

Take a Journey into the World of Crypto and Discover the 3 Keys to Unlock Your Financial Destiny

Damon L Johnson

CLAIM YOUR FREE GIFT!

Your FREE Gift

This guide is best used in conjunction with the best-selling book,
*Deep Into The Bitcoin Rabbit Hole: Take a Journey into the World of
Crypto and Discover the 3 Keys to Unlock Your Financial Destiny.*

If you do not have a copy, then you are in luck. You can grab it
here for FREE:

http://RabbitHoleResourceGuide.com

To have the best experience with *DEEP INTO THE BITCOIN RABBIT HOLE,* I have found that readers who download my free *"Rabbit Hole Resource Guide",* are better able to implement faster and take the next steps needed to begin their journey into the world of cryptocurrency.

You can claim your free guide by visiting:

http://www.RabbitHoleResourceGuide.com

DEDICATION

I dedicate this book to all the youth in my family. May the information in this book inspire the mass adoption of Bitcoin and jumpstart the biggest wealth transfer ever seen in the world.

Jimmy (age 1)

Savion (age 3)

Price (age 5)

Aaliyah (age 7)

Nick (age 7)

Aden (age 10)

Mya (age 11)

Marcelo (age 12)

Brelynn (age 17)

Table of Contents

CLAIM YOUR FREE GIFT!... iii

DEDICATION... iv

DISCLAIMER vi

INTRODUCTION 1

CHAPTER 1 - Meet the Bitcoin Community...................17

#1 – DECENTRALIZATION......................................17

CHAPTER 2 -Wall Street is Coming 33

#2 – PERMISSIONLESS...33

CHAPTER 3- Facebook vs. Government vs. Bitcoin......47

#3 – PSEUDONYMOUS 47

CHAPTER 4- Key #1 – Learn Bitcoin 63

#4 – CENSORSHIP RESISTANT 63

CHAPTER 5- Key #2 – Build and Work in Bitcoin.........77

#5 – IMMUTABLE..77

CHAPTER 6- Key # 3 – Acquire Bitcoin.........................97

#6 – TRANSPARENT...97

CHAPTER 7- Meet the Excellence Academy 113

#7 – DISINFLATIONARY 113

WORKS CITED...127

ABOUT THE AUTHOR 133

THANK YOU FOR READING MY BOOK! 134

DISCLAIMER

I am not an Investment Advisor. This book is for informational, educational, and entertainment purposes only. No information contained in this book constitutes tax, legal, insurance or investment advice.

This book should not be considered a solicitation, offer or recommendation for the purchase or sale of any cryptocurrency, security, or any other financial products and services discussed herein.

Readers of this book should know that Bitcoin is very volatile. You should do your own research before deciding to invest your money and know that you can lose all your money.

Readers of this book should not construe any discussion or information contained herein as personalized advice from the author or the publisher. Readers should discuss the personal applicability of the specific products, services, strategies, or issues posted herein with a professional advisor of his or her choosing.

Information throughout this book, whether asset quotes, charts, articles, or any other statement or statements regarding capital markets or other financial information, is obtained from sources which we, believe reliable, but we do not warrant or guarantee the timeliness or accuracy of this information. Neither our information providers nor we shall be liable for any errors or inaccuracies, regardless of cause, or the lack of timeliness of, or for any delay or interruption in, the transmission thereof to the user. With respect to information regarding financial performance, nothing in this book should be interpreted as a statement or implication that past results are an indication of future performance.

INTRODUCTION

"Compound interest is the eighth wonder of the world.

He who understands it, earns it…He who doesn't…pays it."

– Albert Einstein

"Bitcoin is the nineth wonder of the world.

He who understands it, earns it…He who doesn't…learns it."

– Damon L Johnson

Today is May 13, 2020. The price of bitcoin is $9,269.99 and the market cap is $170.4B.

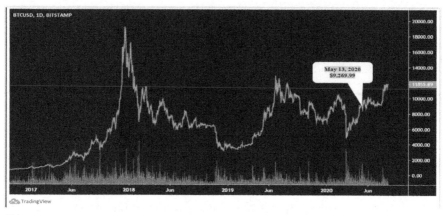

(1)

Hello and welcome! My name is Damon L Johnson and I appreciate this opportunity to share with you my journey into the world of cryptocurrency. May 13, 2020 is the day I began writing this book about my twenty-six-month journey into the world of crypto that started two years earlier. In chapter one, I begin my journey in May of 2018, and by the time we finish the book in chapter seven, we have traveled two years back to the current time of May 2020.

In 2020 Bitcoin is eleven years old, however this relatively new digital currency has yet to gain mainstream awareness and acceptance from the United States public. However, 2018 and 2019 did present some subtle clues in the United States, that told the public that now, more than any other time in the past, is the time to pay attention to Bitcoin and cryptocurrency as a new asset class. We will cover these clues throughout the subsequent chapters. However, in this introduction, we will look at three clues that presented themselves in early 2020.

The first subtle clue came from the US Internal Revenue Service (IRS). Out of nowhere, in January of 2020, the Treasury Department added a mandatory question on the 2019 Schedule 1 of IRS form 1040 that asked,

"At any time during 2019, did you receive, sell, send, exchange or

otherwise acquire any financial interest in any virtual currency?"
(2)

Did you notice that new question? This was a yes/no question, and of course, the IRS wants you to answer the question honestly, but the truth is, it does not matter how you answer this question because it does not affect the result of your tax return. However, the government is quietly telling you that as of 2020, cryptocurrency is now important to the government and we want to know how many people are already ahead of this new financial game.

There are several more subtle clues that presented themselves in 2020, but before I go any farther, I must stop right here and issue a personal warning.

What you are reading may change the way you look at money forever. Once you finish reading this book, your conscience will hold you accountable for your financial future. You will find that some ideas in this book are revolutionary. That is because a technology and monetary revolution is not only coming, but they are already underway. You can consider me your modern-day Paul Revere. I intend for this book to sound an alarm in your spirit because this revolution may not be televised. From this point forward, I put you on notice.

The revolutionary ideas in this book center on the future of money. I know that many of you may be uncomfortable with or do not like change. Therefore, I also know that nine out of ten of you reading this may want to dismiss these ideas immediately. Do not let that be your mistake. You do not want to follow in the footsteps of AOL and Netscape leaders who were presented with a similar warning in the early 90's regarding fiber optics and broadband, nor do you want to make the same mistake as the Blockbuster Video leaders, who heard warnings about an emerging streaming service called Netflix. The fact is that disruptive technology can be lethal if you do not pay attention and heed the warnings. This revolution will be different. It is currently underway slowly but will soon happen all at once. Do not let this new Bitcoin technology leave you behind!

Therefore, this book is for those readers who have visionary leadership. I must admit that the ideas in this book will only sit well with those readers who are comfortable with risk-taking. I hope these characteristics describe you. You see, I envisioned the ideal reader and target audience of this book to be best described as the Main Street investor. This audience contrasts with the savvy financial investors who may be involved in big business and high finance of Wall Street. These savvy Wall Street investors already have a head start and they already know the truth about what I am writing about in this book. I envisioned my Main Street audience to be the ninety-five percent of the US population who have had no or little exposure to Bitcoin or cryptocurrency. You are probably the average US citizen who lives paycheck to paycheck and would probably struggle to come up with $1,000 for an emergency expense. In my mind, a large part of this target audience are women and minorities in the US who have been historically underrepresented in the professional careers of business, finance, and technology. On the other hand, I believe an equal part of this target audience are the new generations of tech-savvy young professionals who are ages 16-36 and may aspire to be entrepreneurs, academics, and thought leaders in the burgeoning digital business and fintech space.

Whoever you are, you will find that this book encourages early adoption of Bitcoin within the rising digital economy. I attempt to specifically demonstrates how the Smart Money (big Institutional Wall Street Investors) are quietly positioning themselves into Bitcoin while the average Main Street investor is being shaken out of the market, is not aware of the market, or is too afraid of the market. However, the silver lining is that this book suggests that it is not too late for the average US citizen to adopt bitcoin, to not only level the playing field in business, technology, and finance, but to win big in the new twenty-first century digital asset economy.

While reading through this book, I hope you feel my authenticity as I guide you through my personal twenty-six-month journey deep into the Bitcoin rabbit hole. You will see that although the subject matter is complex and technical by nature, I write this book in easy to understand language suitable for reading by tech professionals and non-technical grandmas. I write this book from my own personal perspective and personal experience of being a seasoned

African American man entering the digital asset space in early 2018.

However, take note that this book is in no way a comprehensive look at Bitcoin. In this book I share lessons that I have learned along the way that you too can apply to lessen your cryptocurrency learning curve. But for your convenience, along the way I use the hashtag #**RabbitHoleResource** to highlight other various resources and people from the Bitcoin and crypto community who are also working to promote the mass adoption of Bitcoin and those who also can provide a more in dept or technical view on various aspects of Bitcoin and the cryptocurrency ecosystem. I encourage you to do further independent research and to follow these individuals and companies on social media or do other due diligence to complete your research. I have also created a free companion guide called *Rabbit Hole Resource Guide*, which details the resources that I highlight throughout this book.

I chose to write *Deep into the Bitcoin Rabbit Hole* for my readers because I know that it will be the readers of today who will set the financial course of the future and decide the financial opportunities that my grandchildren will have when they grow up. I believe that between now and then (2020 – 2040), a new class of wealth will be created due to the mass adoption of bitcoin and digital finance and I reiterate that it is not too late for Main Street investors to join this digital revolution. I do not want my readers to miss out on this early adopter advantage.

Now let us get back to the subtle clues that 2020 is presenting that tells us that now is the time to be aware of and understand cryptocurrencies such as bitcoin. Were you aware that the Office of the Comptroller of the Currency (OCC) announced that Brian P. Brooks will become its next Chief Operating Officer and First Deputy Comptroller, effective April 1, 2020? (3) This was significant because the OCC is the federal agency that charters, regulates, and supervises all national banks and federal savings associations as well as federal branches and agencies of foreign banks. The OCC is an independent bureau of the US Department of the Treasury. What makes this appointment noteworthy is the fact that Brian Brooks joins the OCC from Coinbase, Inc., where he had served as

Chief Legal Officer since September 2018. Coinbase is a US cryptocurrency exchange that was founded in 2012. This means that the head of all national banks is a Bitcoiner.

To prove this fact, on July 22, 2020, the OCC issued a press release that said that all federally chartered banks and thrifts may now provide custody services for crypto assets. (4) That means that your local bank can now store your bitcoin and cryptocurrency for you. But remember, right now, very few people even know what cryptocurrency is. We are still exceedingly early. What you should know however, is that the government, big institutions, and Smart Money investors know what Bitcoin is and they know of its importance and they are positioning themselves to benefit from it before the masses of the public comes to know this little secret.

Why do I say we are early? Well, as I mentioned from the start, On May 13, 2020, bitcoin's current market cap is $170.4B. The market cap is basically the value of money flowing through the Bitcoin network at any given time. I consider bitcoin's market cap as a key indicator as to where we are in the adoption cycle of Bitcoin. According to my calculations, at $170B, we are still exceedingly early.

I am in the technology field by profession, and while researching Bitcoin, I came across the technology adoption life cycle. I then compared where I felt Bitcoin was along the adoption curve. Below is a chart that I created of the technology adoption life cycle. You see the adoption curve starts slowly, then ramps up fast before it levels off and comes back down. However, over time, the bitcoin market cap will just continue to increase until bitcoin takes all the share of global money and becomes the global reserve and only necessary currency. In the Bitcoin community we call this phenomenon hyperbitconization.

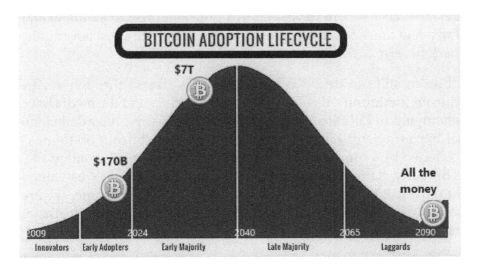

Therefore, I put the bitcoin market cap of $170.4B in the Early Adopters stage. Although $170.4B may seem like an impressive amount of money, this is just a drop in the bucket compared to other asset classes and the total money supply in the world. For instance, economic experts say that the gold market has about a $7 trillion value. You will find that Bitcoin experts refer to bitcoin as digital gold, therefore, until bitcoin gets to a market cap of $7 trillion, I say it is still an early stage investment. However, know that skeptics disagree with me and say that Bitcoin is another tech bubble and it will eventually go back to zero. My response to the critics is,

> *"Look at the scoreboard, Bitcoin ($170.4B). We are still early. Bitcoin still not dead."* – Damon L Johnson

As of today, in 2020, the Bitcoin network is 11 years old and only a select group of people understand it, use it, and own it. According to a Wells Fargo / Gallup poll (5), only about two percent of US investors say they currently own bitcoin, and I personally believe that number is probably a lot less than that. Less than one percent say they plan to buy it soon. While most investors say they have no interest in ever buying bitcoin, about twenty-six percent say they are intrigued by it but will not be buying it anytime soon. It is true that the innovator investors who came super early to Bitcoin between 2009 – 2016 have seen this little asset rise to a bubble and fall a few times but it keeps surviving and the price has never gone back to zero.

"Bitcoin still not dead" is a meme that is shared throughout the Bitcoin community. It was started because critics and the media have attempted to kill Bitcoin off several times. The first recorded claim of bitcoin's demise was in 2010, on a blog of "bitcoin obituaries" collected by a company called 99Bitcoins, a bitcoin information site. This early claim of bitcoin's death came when bitcoin was valued at only $0.23. It is now worth more than $9,000. Trust me, we are still early. The site, 99Bitcoins, has tracked a total of 350 deaths of bitcoin, the most recent of which was made on March 4, 2020.

> *"If you wanna buy Bitcoin, be prepared to lose all your money. If you wanna buy — buy it, but understand what's you've got. It has no intrinsic value"* (6)

That death pronouncement was made by Andrew John Bailey, a British central banker who has been Governor of the Bank of England since March 16, 2020. I think he may be a little bias.

When I look out at the next twenty years, I believe that there is a fifty percent chance that bitcoin or another digital asset will become the world's global reserve currency, replacing the US dollar, or at worst, existing side by side in the existing traditional finance market. This is why I believe you have central bankers like Andrew John Bailey and other traditional finance leaders trying to kill Bitcoin. They see it as a threat to the status quo of traditional finance where they make all the rules and reap all the benefits.

I further believe that within the next twenty years, just as every company is a technology company now because of the internet, by 2040, every company will be a digital asset company because of Bitcoin and blockchain technology. By 2040, we should be at the top of the Bitcoin adoption curve. The late majority will just be getting into bitcoin. By then, bitcoin will have totally replaced gold as the main store of value asset, making it truly digital gold 2.0. and bitcoin's market cap will be greater or equal to $7 Trillion. It may sound crazy now, but I am going to go out on a limb and say that by 2040, the price of bitcoin will have reached a price between $1 million and $10 million.

As I see it, between the years of 2020 - 2040, the mass adoption of Bitcoin and other digital assets, will create a new class of wealth for the current and incoming generations of new financial investors and entrepreneurs. As a result of the actions from these early adopters, I believe that the United States will see its first trillionaires.

Based on the anecdotal evidence that I see in 2020, these firsts trillionaires are likely to be the savvy financial investors within big business and high finance of Wall Street and/or the early crypto company startup founders like the **#RabbitHoleResourse** – Winklevoss brothers, Cameron and Tyler, cofounders of Gemini Cryptocurrency Exchange. The Winklevoss twins are rumored to hold about one percent of the total bitcoin supply, and still accumulating. (7)

However, it is my contention that it is not too late for the average Main Street citizen to also join the twenty-first century digital revolution as early adopter investors and entrepreneurs to experience the exponential value that this new digital asset class will create. All the average citizen needs is a proper introduction and education to Bitcoin and the crypto world.

By now you may be asking yourself several questions: "What is Bitcoin? Is it a good time to invest in Bitcoin? Why is it important? Why do I need it?" Hopefully, the answer to these questions will become clear as you follow my journey into the crypto world. But for now, I will start you off with a quick cliff note version to help you better understand Bitcoin. As you read through the main chapters of this book, you will get a more in depth feel on the answer to your questions.

Bitcoin is many things to different people, but basically Bitcoin is a monetary system. Bitcoin is a better form of money to facilitate twenty-first century commerce. Bitcoin is sound money and currently functions mostly as a good store of value. Many people refer to bitcoin as gold 2.0. However, in future stages of bitcoin, I believe that it will also serve as the best medium of exchange and unit of account. In all monetary properties such as scarcity, durability, fungibility, divisibility, and transferable; bitcoin is superior to fiat money in all those categories.

Bitcoin is a technology platform. Bitcoin is an emerging technology that is quietly disrupting various industries around the world, especially in the financial services industry. Bitcoin cannot be stopped or controlled by any government. With Bitcoin you are self-sovereign and can be your own bank. Just realize that being your own bank requires personal responsibility and accountability because Bitcoin does not have a CEO and there is no customer support line. Bitcoin is fully decentralized.

Bitcoin has been the best investment asset in the last ten years. But trading bitcoin is exceedingly difficult. The bitcoin market is volatile. In 2019 the price of bitcoin was $14K and $3.5K in the same year. Unless you are a professional trader, I do not advise trading bitcoin. I follow the strategy of buying and holding. I am what they call in the crypto community, a long-term HODLer (rhymes with 'bottler' -- more on that later).

Unfortunately, bitcoin is very misunderstood by those looking in from the outside. More than likely, you were probably told that bitcoin was for drug dealers. Bitcoin is only used by terrorist and money launders. Bitcoin uses too much energy and it is killing the planet and the polar bears. All those things may be true, but I will assure you that this portrayal of bitcoin is not the full story.

If you want a true portrayal of bitcoin, you must get it from those who are on the inside. We on the inside, passionately defend bitcoin because we believe that it is the best form of money the world has ever known. This twenty-first century system of internet money is:

1. Decentralized
2. Permissionless
3. Pseudonymous
4. Censorship Resistant
5. Immutable
6. Transparent
7. Disinflationary

It serves the needs of global commerce for everyone anytime and anywhere. I call these the **7 Superpowers of Bitcoin**, and I highlight one of each of the superpowers at the beginning of each chapter.

Okay, for now, let us continue with a brief recap of some Bitcoin history and milestones.

- A person or group of people, with the pseudonym of Satoshi Nakamoto, published the Bitcoin whitepaper 10/31/2008.
- The Bitcoin Network officially launched and mined its first block on 1/3/2009.
- Laszlo Hanyecz buys 2 pizzas for 10,000 bitcoin on 5/22/2010 (Bitcoin Pizza Day).
- Satoshi Nakamoto makes a public post on a cypherpunk electronic mailing list for the last time and disappears 12/12/2010.

(8)

Let us now deal with capital "B"itcoin versus lower case "b"itcoin. Bitcoin is many things to different people. It is a technology protocol, a currency, a new asset class.

- Capital Bitcoin is the technology network. It is the base layer of a technology protocol for the decentralized peer-to-peer network that creates consensus without needing a central authority to prove trust. Other technologies can be built upon this protocol stack like how http, and TCP/IP are a part of the internet protocol stack.
- Lower case bitcoin is the currency. It is the token issued as a reward to miners and made as a tradable asset within the Bitcoin network.

  - The currency bitcoin is both singular and plural. You can have one bitcoin, or you can have one-hundred bitcoin.

  - A bitcoin can be divided into eight decimal places. You see, there is a big misconception. You do not have to buy a full bitcoin. So that means that you can buy them in fractions called satoshis (sats for short). As the price of bitcoin continues to rise, satoshis will become the standard because the price of one bitcoin will soon be out of the reach for the average retail consumer.

	bitcoin	satoshi
1 bitcoin is	1	100,000,000
1 satoshi is	0.00000001	1

(8)

I speculate that the Bitcoin network was originally created for the average Main Street citizen. When Bitcoin was launched on January 3, 2009, the world was at the height of the global financial crisis, which was caused by the big banks of Wall Street. Most Bitcoin enthusiast, such as I, will say that Bitcoin was launched in direct response to this failure of the traditional Wall Street financial system. My fellow Bitcoin enthusiast will say that Bitcoin was positioned as the "People's" money – an alternative financial system.

Even according to Merriam-Webster dictionary,

Definition of Bitcoin

: a digital currency created for use in peer-to-peer online transactions

Introduced in 2008 by a person or group using the name Satoshi Nakamoto, Bitcoin is the most prominent of a group of virtual currencies—money that exists mainly as computer code—that have no central issuing authority.

— Carter Dougherty

… Bitcoin … is backed by no government and has a fluctuating value linked in part to a scarcity that is mathematically predetermined.

— Glenn Zorpette

The venture capital industry is beginning to take a good, hard look at a new financial instrument coming out of the bitcoin community — Initial Coin Offerings, or ICOs.

   — Richard Kastelein

also usually bitcoin

: a unit of this currency

Commercial space venture Virgin Galactic—which announced on Nov. 22 that it would start accepting bitcoins to reserve a refundable $250,000 seat on a future trip—is just the latest of many businesses that have recently embraced the decentralized virtual payment system. (At press time, 1 bitcoin was worth roughly $879.)

   — Time

(9)

As I see it, the Bitcoin network was supposed to be an alternative financial system that offered the people a twenty-first century financial innovation in the form of digital internet money, and from 2009 – 2017, the Bitcoin network did just that. However, when we fast forward to the beginning of 2018, the cryptocurrency market began to take a new turn. Of course, this was just as I began to enter the market. Instead of serving as an alternative financial system for the average citizen of Main Street like me, Bitcoin and other cryptocurrency projects began to receive interest from the big money institutional investors of Wall Street, while the little Main Street investors began to lose confidence in bitcoin and exited the market.

The rumors began that "The herd is coming", a phrase coined by billionaire CEO of Galaxy Digital, Michael Novogratz, and it was true. The Smart Money, as I call them, began to quietly positional themselves into Bitcoin and other cryptocurrency projects, as they entered the space as venture capitalist investing into startup crypto companies and crypto funds that would eventually go on to be responsible for building this new infrastructure and foundation for the new global digital asset economy that is developing before our eyes. The Smart Money knew something that the average citizens did not know.

This brings me to my third and final subtle clue that I say that 2020 has given us, to tell the public, you should be paying attention to Bitcoin and cryptocurrency. According to a report from *The Block*, Texas has become the home of three huge bitcoin mining farms due to Texas' abundant and cheap energy sources. You can picture a mining farm as a big data center full of dedicated computers, whose only responsibility is to issue bitcoin into circulation. These mining farms were built to compete with China's dominance in bitcoin mining. *The Block* reports that Whinstone (a Louisiana-based developer of high-speed data centers) and Northern Bitcoin (a Germany-based bitcoin mining firm) announced that they merged to open a 100-acre bitcoin mining farm in the state of Texas. They further said that the mining farm would be the "largest bitcoin mining facility worldwide with a capacity of one gigawatt."

> *"With this merger, we are catapulting ourselves faster than original-ly planned to the top of the world in bitcoin mining. Together, we have a dominant leadership position in this fast-growing industry and are well-positioned to benefit significantly from the future development of blockchain technology,"*

said Mathis Schultz, CEO of Northern Bitcoin AG.

Similarly, *The Block* reports that Chinese crypto mining hardware giant Bitmain launched a 50-megawatt mining farm, also in Texas.

The Block also reports that Digital Currency Group (DCG)-backed firm Layer1 also recently raised $50 million to build mining chips and to run its own electricity substations in Texas and to that end, the firm bought a dozen acres of land in the city. (10)

Now on the surface, you would think that the injection of hundreds of millions of dollars into the cryptocurrency ecosystem, provided by the Wall Street investors, was a positive development because it would lead to market cap growth and price appreciation in the crypto markets, which in turn would attract new average retail investors, further growing the market cap and causing more price appreciation. However, as an average middle class, African American man entering the crypto world as a retail investor in this new digital finance economy, I began to see some problems that troubled me. The alternative financial system that drew me in, was beginning to closely mirror some bad characteristic of its traditional financial system counterpart.

As it related to the mass adoption of Bitcoin, I saw three main issues that were problematic (We will explore these issues in chapters 1 -3):

- Problem 1 – The big money institutional investors of Wall Street were coming in while at the same time, the average Main Street investor, like me, was being shaken out of the market due to the extreme price volatility.
- Problem 2 – The Wealth Inequality Gap was widening – as like the traditional financial system, the Bitcoin and digital asset space was being polarized by the one percent of the "Haves", who hold ninety percent or more of the US crypto wealth and the ninety-nine percent of the "Have Nots", who hold less than ten percent of the U.S crypto wealth.
- Problem 3 – The Diversity, Equity, & Inclusion was lacking – As like within the traditional financial system, women and marginalized minority groups were being underrepresented in the new digital asset economy. I did not see of any women or minority bitcoin miners in the US and very few women or minorities who served in leading roles in US cryptocurrency companies.

As a result of these problematic issues, I felt an immediate need to do something that would help reverse these trends. I knew that I was on the right road when I found Bitcoin and I did not want to take this journey by myself. Remember, mass adoption of Bitcoin is the key to success, but I want to see more people who look and feel like me along the journey. Of course, there were a few examples of Black people like me succeeding in the space, and I highlight them along the way with the hashtag #**BlackExcellence**. These were people, who were, or can in the future, make a great impact along the Bitcoin mass adoption journey. I also highlight and detail these resources in my free companion guide *Rabbit Hole Resource Guide*.

I do not know about you but, I am following the lead of the Smart money, so I am sure that I am on the right path. I believe that the solution starts with providing a proper Bitcoin and crypto introduction/reintroduction and education to other average Main Street citizens, along with the current and incoming generations of new women and minority investors who have been historically left behind in the traditional financial markets.

 Therefore, my goal for this book is to illuminate these problems that I saw, show how they came to be, then show the impact that they are currently having. I do this throughout the first three chapters of the book. Beginning in chapter four through six, I demonstrate that the fix to these problems can be 3 Key solutions (L.A.B): Learning Bitcoin, Acquiring Bitcoin, Building in the Bitcoin ecosystem. I finish the book by introducing you to my family business and new startup company, SoFL Excellence Academy. Our company offers you a platform that you can utilize as next steps along your own personal journey into the world of Bitcoin and cryptocurrency.

After you have read this book and download my free companion guide, I promise you that you will be able to empower yourselves to choose whether you want to be a part of the "Haves", and experience the exponential wealth creation that Bitcoin and digital finance will create, or you can choose to be a part of the "Have Nots", and let your early adopter advantage expire as you live with the current status quo. With this introduction and education to Bitcoin, at least the choice is yours.

CHAPTER 1

Meet the Bitcoin Community

The 7 Superpowers of Bitcoin:

#1 – DECENTRALIZATION

Decentralization is Bitcoin's power to distribute power away from any central authority within Bitcoin's peer-to-peer network of globally connected computer nodes. Each node maintains a complete copy of the blockchain and contributes to the functioning and security of the network. Satoshi Nakamoto designed Bitcoin as a decentralized alternative to government-controlled money. Therefore, Bitcoin does not have any single point of failure, making it more resilient, efficient, and democratic. Its underlying technology, the blockchain, is what allows for this decentralization, as it offers every single user the opportunity to become one of the network's many payment validators and processors.

Happy birthday to me! Today is May 10, 2018 and it is my 50th birthday. The price for a full bitcoin is $9,043.94 and bitcoin's market cap is $154.0B. We are still early. Bitcoin still not dead.

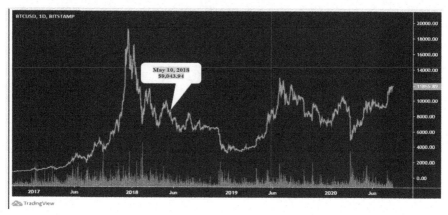

(1)

As of today, May 10, 2018, I have been in the crypto market for a little over 2 months. I am celebrating my 50th birthday at a steak house in West Hollywood, and all I can think about is, "How did I miss the Bull Run of 2017?" This was the time in 2017 when the price of bitcoin spiked from $1,003 on January 1 to $20,059 on December 17. That was a yearly increase of 1,900%. The price went from $10K to $20K in only eighteen days in that December.

Since then, the price has come back down about fifty percent, so I am thinking that I chose a great level to jump into the action. However, at this point, I really did not understand that bitcoin was digital gold, nor did I care about any of the 7 Superpowers that make Bitcoin so innovative and revolutionary. There were several great books and resources out there to help you understand Bitcoin from a technical and economic standpoint but none of that really mattered right then. I was in it for greed and pure speculation. I was an experienced stock and options trader, so asset investing was not new to me. However, this seemed a little different. I was excited about this new financial opportunity that I found and I knew that it would only be a matter of time before the price of bitcoin would get back up to its all-time high of $20k and surpass it. That would be more than a double of my initial investment.

However, there was one big problem that I saw in 2018. Simply put, I felt that not enough average citizens had been introduced and educated to Bitcoin or other digital finance assets, especially women and minorities like me who have been historically left behind in the traditional financial investing markets. As I saw it, over the next twenty or so years, I expected that the mass adoption of bitcoin and other digital assets, would create a new class of wealth for the current and incoming generations of new financial investors and entrepreneurs. I honestly believed that the average citizen investor was at risk of missing this great financial opportunity if no one informed and prepared the masses.

Therefore, it was my contention that it is not too late for the average citizen of Main Street to join the twenty-first century digital revolution as early adopter investors and entrepreneurs to experience the exponential value that this new digital asset class will create. All the average Main Street investor needed was for someone to provide them with a proper introduction and education to Bitcoin and the crypto world.

You're Welcome!

Well, you may be asking, how did I get started on my journey down the Bitcoin rabbit hole? As like many other average Main Street citizens in the Bitcoin and digital asset space, my introduction and education was a solo activity, only seeing a few friends and peers along the way. You see after the Bull Run of 2017, many cryptocurrency "experts" and analysts, who had financial advice newsletters, tried to help the Bitcoin adoption problem. They all began to heavily promote Bitcoin through their services, and as a person who was previously on many "Make Money from Home" lists, I became a prime target of their advertising. However, it did not matter, because I was used to sending most of those email ads to the trash. Trust me, I had seen every scam and legitimate offer out there and nothing really interested me in the last couple of years with the exception of real estate, and unfortunately, I was just recovering from a real estate deal gone bad.

I am not sure exactly what it was that hooked me, but when I was introduced to the idea of Bitcoin, it clicked right away. I knew this opportunity was different than any other I had been presented in the past. The interesting thing was that I had already heard of Bitcoin five years earlier in 2013, when I was looking into starting an internet business. However, I only knew Bitcoin to be an alternative payment processor option for your website if PayPal would not work with your internet business model. I remember slightly looking into Bitcoin back then but then I dropped it because I really did not understand how I could use this "magical internet money" in the real world. I had no idea that you could invest or trade bitcoin like the stock market. Oh, how I wish I could go back to that time and revisit that research. Bitcoin was only $117.20 on May 10, 2013 and based on the amount of bitcoin that I have today in 2020, I could have had 91.5412969 bitcoin today, which would be worth $887,150!

When I came across Bitcoin in early 2018, it was introduced to me by **#RabbitHoleResource** - Teeka Tiwari. He was one of the cryptocurrency experts that was pitching Bitcoin. He worked for the Palm Beach Research Group. Teeka was the editor of their flagship service *The Palm Beach Letter* and their cryptocurrency advisory called *Palm Beach Confidential*. Teeka was a former hedge fund manager and Wall Street executive so I felt that he came with some credibility. I was on guard and looking out for any scammers because there were plenty of them coming around as well.

I listened to Teeka speak on a webinar (11) and he was very convincing that bitcoin would be one of the greatest investments we would see in 2018. I think this is what grabbed my attention. Teeka pointed to the almost 2,000% rise in bitcoin in 2017, but he said that 2018 had the potential to be even more transformational.

After listening to Teeka's webinar, I found three compelling reasons to purchase my first satoshi (the base unit of account in a bitcoin). You see, there is a big misconception. You do not have to buy a full bitcoin. Bitcoin is divisible out to eight decimal places. So that means that you can buy them in fractions called satoshis.

The first compelling reason Teeka gave was pure speculation and I know he used it to make people act quickly to his pitch. He pointed to the fact that Amazon's quarterly earnings was approaching within the next month and he speculated that if Amazon were to announce that they were now accepting bitcoin on their ecommerce platform, that news would skyrocket the price of bitcoin. At the time, that speculation sounded plausible. Eventually we would see that did not happen, at least not that quarter.

The second compelling point Teeka made was that a tidal wave of institutional money was heading into bitcoin. He gave actual evidence that it had already started. He noted that the Chicago Mercantile Exchange (CME) and the Chicago Board of Options Exchange (CBOE) had recently launched bitcoin futures and option products and massive institutional Wall Street money was beginning to flow into bitcoin. However, Teeka said that the CME and CBOE would pave the way for an even bigger event.

The bigger event was the third compelling reason. This event would be the eventual launch of a bitcoin exchange traded fund (ETF). He said that an ETF would make it as easy to buy bitcoin as it is to buy a stock, with just one click of your mouse and that this would usher in a brand-new wave of average retail investors. You see in 2018, it was still a pain to buy bitcoin from most places and even harder to buy other cryptocurrencies, but an ETF would solve that problem. Teeka said that once we got a Bitcoin ETF, bitcoin could easily go up to $100,000 per coin based on supply and demand. He predicted that bitcoin was going to become a portion of just about everyone's asset allocation. The only problem is that there is just not enough bitcoin to go around, and this is a good thing!

Teeka described how bitcoin had a fixed supply of 21 million coins and that about 16.7 million bitcoin were already mined into the circulating supply up to that point. However, of that 16.7 million, about 5 million bitcoin have been lost, which only leaves about 11.7 million bitcoin left in circulation. He went on to explain that there are about 35 million millionaires in the world and most of them are going to want a bitcoin in their portfolio once bitcoin became mainstream and everyone is talking about it on CNBC. However, there lies the problem. There is not enough bitcoin in circulation for every millionaire to have just one. The point of his argument was that supply and demand will kick in as everyone tries to squeeze into the bitcoin market at the last minute, and the price will skyrocket once it became that easy to purchase. His whole point was that the ordinary retail investor should get in early now before the crowd comes and while the price and market cap are still relatively low.

Teeka was not the only crypto analyst who was predicting a massive rise in bitcoin's price. In an article called "Top 10 Expert Bitcoin Price Predictions for 2018 & Beyond", Wilma Woo cited several well-respected voices in the crypto and finance space as they weighed in with their price predictions. (12)

Thomas Lee: $25,000

"We still think Bitcoin can reach $25,000 by the end of the year or something like that." – Thomas Lee. Lee is the founder of research company FundStart Global.

Max Keiser: $28,000 – $100,000

"The move to $28,000 will be crisis-driven and then no Bitcoin will be available under $100,000 as price gaps – and even at that price, not much BTC available." – Max Keiser.

David Drake $30,000

"I'd say this year is a cryptocurrency Wall Street time and … we think cryptocurrency on the Bitcoin will be worth $30,000 at the year-end—it is limited." – David Drake. Drake is the founder of LDJ Capital.

Jeet Singh: $50,000

"Bitcoin could definitely see $50,000… We will probably go through a suffering period of volatility around the time of Bitcoin's next $10,000 landmark." – Jeet Singh. Singh's prediction was made in January at the World Economic Forum.

Bobby Lee: $60,000

"When Bitcoin passes the USD $60,000 price level in the coming

years, it'll reach a total circulation value of $1 Trillion. That will be a huge milestone for $BTC, and it'll lead to more price stability, higher global liquidity, and even faster adoption worldwide. VirtuousCycle" – Bobby Lee. Lee, the head of the Bitcoin Foundation said, prices could climb as high as $1 million.

Vinny Lingham: $100,000 – $1Million

"Bitcoin currently is priced at 2.5% chance of being worth $100k or .25% chance of being worth $1m." – Vinny Lingham. Lingham is a co-founder of Civic and a member of the Bitcoin Foundation.

Tim Draper $250,000

"This is going to be so big so if you see a dip, jump in. Maybe it will dip further but boy, I made that prediction and I'm sticking to it. $250,000 by 2022 for Bitcoin." – Tim Draper. Draper is the founder of Draper Associates and DFJ.

Cameron Winklevoss $320,000

"So, if you look at a $100 billion market cap today, now last week it might have been more like 200, so it's actually a buying opportunity, we think that there's a potential appreciation of 30 to 40 times because you look at the gold market today, it's a $7 trillion market. And so, a lot of people are starting to see that, they recognize the store of value properties. So, we think regardless of the price moves in the last few weeks, it's still a very underappreciated asset." – Cameron Winklevoss.

John Pfeffer $700,000

"Bitcoin is the first viable candidate to replace gold the world has ever seen. So, if Bitcoin becomes the dominant non-sovereign store of value, it could be the new gold, or new reserve currency." – John Pfeffer.

John McAfee $1 Million

"I absolutely stand by the million-dollar prediction…It is still two and a half years away, in which two things will happen: Bitcoin will continue to grow, and the US dollar and other fiat currencies will

devalue." – John McAfee.

As I continued my early journey into Bitcoin and crypto, I realized early that bitcoin was not just a US currency. Instead, it was a global currency and asset and that there were so many voices speaking about the pros and cons of bitcoin. I knew that if I really wanted to participate in this growing asset class, I would have to first educate myself and get acquainted with the Bitcoin and crypto online communities.

The first lesson I learned was that Bitcoin has financially conservative values. It really appeals to Libertarian thought. In the Bitcoin finance world, you must take personal responsibility for all your actions. By its nature, Bitcoin is not controlled by any government or any centralized entity due to its decentralization. Therefore, there are no government safety nets or insurance if you get scammed or you lose your digital keys to your assets. Therefore, I knew I would have to follow the crypto community's mantra, "Do Your Own Research". That is every newbie's command.

In the crypto world, you realize quickly that you do not just believe every guy you hear on the internet, just because he has an opinion. However, I did begin my education on the internet. I introduced myself to the Crypto Twitter, Crypto YouTube, and Crypto Podcast communities. I weeded through several Twitter feeds, YouTube channels, and crypto podcasts until I found the crypto influencers that gave credible and reliable information. I found these three platforms to be very insightful.

Crypto Twitter was the most amusing community, but it was incredibly valuable as well. It was the quickest way to get the current crypto news. One moment you are Scrolling through the latest crypto memes, while the next moment you get a tweet from the CEO of Twitter on how he is all in on Bitcoin. Imagine that, **#RabbitHoleResource -** Jack Dorsey, who is the CEO of Twitter and Square, is a Bitcoiner. Through Square's Cash App, Jack just made it easier for everyday people to buy and store bitcoin.

(13)

To this day, I make it a point to check in on Crypto Twitter multiple times per day. It is the first thing that I do every day. I follow such crypto Twitter greats as:

#RabbitHoleResource -

- Pomp @APompliano – Cofounder & partner at Morgan Creek Digital
- Dan Hedl @danheld – Business Development officer at Kraken
- Matt Senter @MattSenter – CTO and Co-Founder of Lolli
- Matt Odell @matt_odell – Bitcoin O.G.
- Peter McCormack @PeterMcCormack – Crypto podcaster
- Barry Silbert @barrysilbert – Founder/CEO Digital Currency Group, Greyscale Investments
- Catherine Coley @cryptocoley – CEO Binance America

- Whale Panda @WhalePanda – Angel Invesor, Crypto O.G.
- CZ Binance @cz_binance – CEO Binance
- Tone Vays @ToneVays – Derivative Trader, Analyst
- Cameron Winklevoss @winklevoss – Cofounder Gemini
- Crypto Bobby @crypto_bobby – Founder Proof of Talent
- The Crypto Dog @TheCryptoDog – Bitcoin O.G.
- Marty Bent @MartyBent – Bitcoin O.G.
- Andreas Antonopoulos @aantonop – Bitcoin O.G.

And the list goes on, everyone from the smartest minds in the digital asset space to the most comical.

I am a little more selective on Crypto YouTube. This is where I get my longer form news. I follow crypto YouTubers that give daily crypto news recaps. Most videos range from ten – forty minutes per day to some YouTubers that do three videos per day or one-hour livestreams.

My favorite YouTube subscriptions are the following:

#RabbitHoleResource –

- The Crypto Sphere with Dvir
- The Gentlemen of Crypto with Bitcoin Zay & King
- Mr. Kristof with Kris
- CNBC Crypto Trader with Ran Neuner
- Tone Vays with Tone Vays

I am the most selective on my crypto podcasts. When I want to hear a deep dive conversation on a crypto topic, I choose my podcasters. On these episodes I got to learn from interviews of the smartest minds in Bitcoin, business, finance, and technology in general.

My podcast library consists of:

#RabbitHoleResource -

- The Pomp Podcast – Anthony Pompliano
- Tales from the Crypt – Marty Bent
- What Bitcoin Did – Peter McCormack
- Once Bitten – Daniel Prince
- Block Stars – David Schwartz

Once you immerse yourself in the crypto community you soon realize that crypto has a unique culture. It has a quirky language, and it is driven by memes. You may have heard the term "Bitcoin maximalism" on crypto podcasts or on Crypto Twitter. It is a term that has evolved from a community that is fierce in its ideological and technological principles. In general, I divide the crypto community into 3 sub-groups based on the coins or digital assets that they support or hold.

1. Bitcoin Maximalist Community – The Bitcoin maximalist community believes with unwavering conviction that Bitcoin is the only cryptocurrency. In fact, they believe bitcoin is the only currency worth caring about. Most maximalists also feel strongly that altcoins (any cryptocurrency that is not Bitcoin) are technically flawed, and morally questionable.

2. Altcoin Community – The Altcoin community supports altcoins. We use the term altcoin to refer to any cryptocurrency that is not bitcoin. This is because these other coins were formed as "alternative coins" to Bitcoin. Most altcoins were created with different goals than bitcoin. Some were built to tackle issues in the finance industry, others may be tailored to disrupting various sectors or functions, like storage or supply chain. Some altcoins were created purely for fun. Dodgecoin, for example, was created for no real purpose.

3. Shitcoin Community – The Shitcoin community is generally made up of speculators and traders. Shitcoin is a pejorative term used to describe an altcoin that was created just as a "money grab" and has since become worthless. Shitcoin value may erode because interest failed to materialize because the altcoin itself was not created in good faith, or because the price was based on speculation. We often identify shitcoins by a specific pattern that they follow. First, the coin launches with a lot of interest, but the price does not do much. However, then, the price increases exponentially over a short period of time as more investors pour in. Finally, the price nosedives, as investors dump their coins to capitalize on short-term gains. The shitcoin speculators and traders know exactly how to take advantage of this volatility.

that many people straddle one or two of these sub communities. One binding characteristics of these sub communities is its quirky language. It is common for these sub communities to communicate with each other in memes and their own special crypto slang.

In the mid to late part of 2018, when the crypto community was suffering through what would really become a two-year bear market, you could not go through a Twitter feed or Reddit thread without someone asking, "When moon?" or "When lambo?". Usually, this was just people being funny and inquiring about when the price of a crypto asset will begin to skyrocket "to the moon" so that they could purchase their Lamborghini (lambo).

Aside from the humorous memes and slang, you also have some serious memes and slang that crypto enthusiast uses every day. You will find that I use the following terms below throughout this book.

According to community submissions in the Binance Academy Glossary:

*"**FUD** – The expression "Fear, uncertainty, and doubt" (FUD) describes the act of spreading dubious or false information about a business, startup, or cryptocurrency project. The term is also used to describe a set of negative sentiment that spreads around traders and investors when bad news comes out or when the market presents a strong bearish down trend."*

*"**HODL** – is a term commonly used by cryptocurrency investors that refuse to sell their cryptocurrency regardless of the price increasing or decreasing. It is more frequently used during a bear market when people refuse to sell their coins despite the price drop. HODL was later retrofitted to be an acronym (backronym) for "Hold On for Dear Life" and refers to not selling, even during strong market volatility and poor market performance."*

*"**BUIDL** – is a warping of the word "build" in the same fashion as "HODL." BUIDL is a call to arms for building and contributing to the blockchain and cryptocurrency ecosystem, instead of passively holding."*

*"**Stack'n Sats** – is a term commonly used within the bitcoin*

community to describe the act of regularly accumulating bitcoin, by buying, earning, or mining. A satoshi is the smallest unit of a bitcoin. It equals one-hundred-millionth of a bitcoin or 0.00000001 BTC. As such, one bitcoin equals 100 million satoshi. The satoshi was named as an homage to the anonymous creator or creators behind Bitcoin, Satoshi Nakamoto. The satoshi is often abbreviated as sat."

"**Bag holder** –in the crypto space, the word bag refers to the coins and tokens one is holding as part of their portfolio. Typically, the term is used to describe a significant amount of a particular cryptocurrency. There is no defined minimum, but when the value is relatively high, one could say they are holding "heavy bags" of a certain coin or token."

"**Nocoiner** – is someone who doesn't know anything about crypto and someone who doesn't have any crypto. Nocoiners often have the behavior of being pessimistic about bitcoin, altcoins, and crypto in general, and often express themselves negatively through FUD."

(14)

You have the following meme sayings:

"The virus is spreading"

"Long Bitcoin, Short the Bankers"

"Plan B, when all else fails, there is Bitcoin"

"Number go up"

"When moon? When Lambo?"

"Bitcoin fixes this"

"Falling down the rabbit hole"

"The Red Pill"

It took me about two years of daily crypto engagement but now I can say that I am all in. I know one hundred percent more than I did about Bitcoin and digital assets than I did two years ago, and I am ready to spread the gospel. The crypto community calls this phenomenon "falling down the rabbit hole". I think I fell deep. I changed my whole routine and habits. On my commute to work or through the city, no longer did I listen to music or talk radio. Whenever I was in the car and the radio was on, I was listening to crypto news updates from YouTube or crypto podcast interviews. After two years, I do not even miss music radio stations.

I now have new apps on my phone. I cannot go a day without checking the current cryptocurrency prices on BitScreener or CoinMarketCap. I must track my crypto portfolio performance with my Blockfolio app and when I need to buy some bitcoin I have a choice between my Coinbase, Binance, Cash App, or BlockFi apps. The best apps of all are my apps that give me free bitcoin; Coinmine and Pei. I talk about these apps in more detail in chapter six when I talk about 'Owning Bitcoin'.

I bounced around all the crypto sub communities, but now I believe that I am firmly in the Bitcoin Maximalist camp. I sold pretty much all my altcoins and shitcoins and hold ninety-nine percent of my crypto in bitcoin (although I do still track my old alt coins). I did, however, keep one altcoin just in case we get another big pop in an alt season. I will just keep my one altcoin secured away until the day I can get a 10,000% gain or more on it. This is crypto, where anything and everything is possible.

The 45-year-old black singer/rapper **#BlackExcellence** - Akon is proving anything is possible. Akon announced that he is in the process of building the world's first 'crypto city' — Akon City — in Senegal, West Africa, and the city will feature his namesake crypto-currency called Akoin, which is actually short for Africa Coin, but it coincidently sounds very close to his name Akon. The 10-year project reports to be a 100% crypto-based city with Akoin at the center of transactional life. According to a report by Kevin Helms, Akon City will be set on a 2,000-acre parcel gifted by the Senegalese president. Akon said that the Akoin team's three-part vision is to empower rising entrepreneurs with digital and real-life tools and services and to enable brands to unlock the power of Africa's rising economy. (15)

CHAPTER 2

Wall Street is Coming

The 7 Superpowers of Bitcoin:

#2 – PERMISSIONLESS

Permissionless is Bitcoin's power to be open and public. With this power, users do not require prior approval before creating a bitcoin address and interacting with the network. There is no need for a preapproved list of network participants to gain consensus. Any person, thing, or entity can interact with other members or parties on the network at any time. Each party can choose to run a node on the blockchain and participate in transaction verifications through the mining consensus mechanism. The data on the Bitcoin network is publicly available, and complete copies of the ledgers are stored across the globe in each participating node. This is what makes it hard to censor or hack the Bitcoin Network. Bitcoin does not have a CEO or anyone who controls it, and one can remain relatively anonymous as there is no need for identifying themselves to get an address and perform transactions.

Today is December 15, 2018. The price for a full bitcoin is $3,236.76 and bitcoin's market cap is $56.7B. We are still early. Bitcoin still not dead.

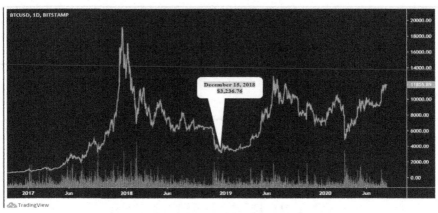

(1)

I have been on my crypto journey for about nine months now and we are currently at the lowest point in the 2018 bear market. Over the last nine months, we have lost over $100B in market cap. I am really starting to hear stories on Twitter of how the little guys are giving up and quitting the crypto market. The price volatility was just too much. A couple months ago, the price of bitcoin was holding steady in the $6,000 range and all the experts were declaring the bottom of the bear market. Then suddenly, the price fell another fifty percent to the $3,000 price range that we currently have in December 2018. What is causing this price destruction? This was the question everyone was asking and fearing. Is bitcoin over?

Bitcoin was down but it was certainly not dead. On the contrary, the fundamentals for Bitcoin were getting stronger despite the drop in price and market cap. I knew for myself that it was time for level heads and to not lose sight of the long-term goal. The prevailing theory on the price drop was that the big institutional investors from Wall Street were purposely driving the prices down so that they could come into the market at lower prices and accumulate as much bitcoin as they can. The institutions were using the derivative products that came online in 2017 that only institutional clients could access, like the bitcoin futures and options, to bet against the price and drive it down.

I considered the drop in crypto prices that we were experiencing, both good and bad. You see by now, I owned seventeen other cryptocurrencies besides bitcoin. I told you, I fell deep down the rabbit hole. This was a brand-new world full of adventure and promise. There were so many cryptocurrency projects that were trying to change the world and make it a better place. Many of them had compelling use cases but the strongest case for me was still speculation. I speculated that the price of these altcoins would spike as so many had done in 2017. For instance, in 2017:

- XRP gained 36,018%
- NEM gained 29,842%
- Ardor gained 16,809%
- Stellar gained 14,441%
- Dash gained 9,265%

(16)

On December 16, 2018, I had the following portfolio of cryptocurrencies:

#	Name	Symbol
1	Bitcoin	BTC
2	Ethereum	ETH
3	Ripple	XRP
4	Bitcoin Cash	BCH
5	Stellar	XLM
6	Litecoin	LTC
7	Dash	DASH
8	Binance Coin	BNB
9	Neo	NEO
10	Ethereum Classic	ETC
11	OmiseGo	OMG
12	Ontology	ONT
13	0x	ZRX
14	Zilliqa	ZIL

15	ICON	ICZ
16	Wanchain	WAN
17	Dragonchain	DRGN
18	Cindicator	CND

At one time, I had confidence in all of these projects however in December of 2018, each of them was down between thirty percent and eighty percent from the price I had originally bought them. But remember I said this price drop was both good and bad news. The bad news was that I eventually decided to take the loss on my altcoins. Therefore, over the next three months, I liquidated out of all my altcoins except for Ripple XRP. I decided to keep this one as a speculative long-term play. If we could get another 36,000% run, like in 2017, my family would be set for a couple of generations.

The good news was that I sold all the proceeds of the altcoins and bought more bitcoin and a little bit more of XRP. While the price of bitcoin continued to go down, I continued to buy more bitcoin. This allowed me to lower my investment cost basis. Therefore, the lower prices helped me out because, just like the big institutional investors were doing, it allowed me to accumulate more coins at the lower prices. We call this buying the dip. I just began to dollar cost average buy a little bit every week. I called this #**Staking-SatsSunday**. You see my goal had changed. Instead of speculating on an altcoin pump, my goal now was to accumulate at least one full bitcoin. If I could do that, I knew that I would be in an exclusive club. Remember, there will only ever be 21 million bitcoin ever in circulation. If you do some statistical math based on the world population of approximately 7.6 billion people, the percentage of people who can own at least one full bitcoin is about 0.2%, and that is if everyone only owned one bitcoin. Many people already own hundreds and some thousands. So that percentage is a lot less. Therefore, owning one full bitcoin truly does put you in an exclusive club over time. As the price of bitcoin continues to rise, satoshis will become the standard. People will accumulate satoshis, but one full bitcoin will eventually become out of reach for the average investor once bitcoin gets to a price of $100,000 and more.

Now let me back up and tell you a little more about my background before I got into Bitcoin. I was born and raised in Cleveland, Ohio and for the last 23 years, I had been working as a financial services professional at one of the largest regional banks in the country. My current role at the bank was as Technology and Database Manager for our Corporate Responsibility division. Over the last nine months, I had been trying to introduce Bitcoin and blockchain to my senior management because everything I was learning was telling me that Bitcoin and cryptocurrency technology could be a major threat to the traditional banking industry. One of the most promising use cases for bitcoin was the ability to bank the more than 2 billion people worldwide who are unbanked or underbanked. I just wanted my management to be aware of this emerging technology because I had not heard any of our executive leaders discussing cryptocurrency or blockchain for that matter.

However, to my surprise, there was a movement in the Cleveland business community to position Cleveland as a hub for blockchain development. A group of business leaders and city officials put together Cleveland's first cryptocurrency conference called Blockland Cleveland and what do you know, my bank was one of the major sponsors. Turns out that our Chief Information Officer (CIO) and several other bank managers were participating and facilitating panel discussions throughout the conference, including my division's executive manager.

Now at this point our bank was still not concerned about bitcoin or crypto. However, they were interested in the blockchain concept. I would just shake my head. All around the country, you hear financial leaders say, "Blockchain not Bitcoin". This was a phrase in the crypto community that drives us crazy. I posed a direct question to my CEO at a townhall meeting and that was his exact reply. He said that he could see the bank having a digital first strategy utilizing the blockchain, however, digital money or having a strategy to compete against digital currency was not on the road map. Imagine that, a bank with a digital first strategy but that strategy does not include money, which is our main product and service. That did not make sense to me, but I think my idea will be vindicated since the OCC has come around and offered clarification that national banks can now custody crypto.

In my opinion, I believe that at that time, the traditional banking executives honestly believe that bitcoin and crypto was just a tool that some investors were using to speculate but it had no real use case in the banking system. However, if you think about it, if blockchain is so great for every other use case, why would it not be great in its first and original use case, bitcoin, digital currency! Time will tell, but I am hedging my bets on bitcoin winning the banking game. We are already seeing evidence that traditional banking is changing, and most banks are reducing the number of physical branches that they have and trying to increase their mobile and web presence. My favorite saying is from an author unknown,

> *"There will always be a need for banking services, but there may not always be a need for banks"* | Unknown

After several conversations and news articles I shared with him, my boss, who was the Director of Community Development, had taken to the idea of cryptocurrency and blockchain. He asked me if I wanted to go to the Blockland Cleveland conference because he could get us tickets at our sponsor rate. I told him, "I am already on the registration page, what is the discount code?" Cleveland was now moving in the right direction. Although this crypto conference was new and not as popular as some others around the country and around the world, for that matter, it did boast a couple of high-profile figures in the crypto community. Notable keynote speakers included #**RabbitHoleResource** - Nick Szabo, who some believe may actually be Satoshi Nakamoto; Joseph Lubin, founder of Consensus Systems (ConsenSys) and co-founder of Ethereum; Larry Sanger, co-founder of Wikipedia; and Alex Tapscott, author of "Blockchain Revolution" and co-founder of Blockchain Research Institute.

Alex Tapscott was the opening night keynote speaker. He gave a great keynote speech explaining how blockchain is the key to creating an internet of value. He encouraged everyone to get involved in the Blockchain Research Institute, one of the leading researchers and think tanks for blockchain technology.

In addition to daily keynote presentations, the conference included tracks of Learning Block sessions in various verticals including banking, finance, insurance, healthcare, government, legal, manufacturing, supply chain logistics, emerging technologies and venture capital as well as workshops and meetups. I had to stop by the workshop facilitated by #**BlackExcellence** – Professor Tanya Evans of the University of New Hampshire School of Law. Professor Evans was one of maybe three black female speakers at the conference. She gave an overview about "Who Needs Blockchain & Why?" (17). This session covered blockchain history, cryptocurrency, and smart contracts basics, and she provide an overview of related legal and regulatory issues. I talked with Professor Evans after the conference and followed her on Crypto Twitter. She is making a name for herself as a Black attorney in the blockchain space.

According to an article by Cleveland.com, (18) the Blockland Solutions cryptocurrency conference did what it said it would do. They had a sold-out crowd, hundreds of developers learning new skills, and highly lauded technology CEOs explaining why blockchain matters and why Cleveland might have a shot at leading the way. The organizers of the events wanted to convince attendees that blockchain was the next phase of the Internet and inspire action. This got me thinking of what I could do in the crypto space. Organizers were preaching that the technology is not just for major companies but that it matters to local manufacturing businesses, entrepreneurs, and technology consultants, too. The Blockland Solutions conference had perfect timing because the Ohio state government had just announced that they were accepting bitcoin for business taxes.

After attending the Blockland Cleveland crypto conference, I was more excited about the prospects of crypto and Bitcoin than ever. I think I realized then that I wanted to start some type of company to support the Bitcoin ecosystem. However, I was a little discouraged because I continued to see the original problem getting bigger. The big guys were coming in, the little guys were leaving out, and the underrepresented women and minorities were being left behind.

One thing for sure that I learned from the conference was that the Smart Money, as I call them, began to quietly positional themselves into Bitcoin and other cryptocurrency projects, as they entered the space as venture capitalist, investing into startup crypto companies and crypto funds that would eventually go on to be responsible for building this new infrastructure and foundation for the new global digital asset economy that is developing before our eyes.

It was no doubt that Wall Street and the Smart Money had their aim set squarely on the crypto market. The Wall Street giants began to get into position and the race had begun. I likened it to a game of musical chairs. These smart investors know that the supply of bitcoin is limited and when the music stops, they do not want to be the last man standing without a chair.

Look at the following news headlines that came out in 2018:

"JP Morgan Files Patent for Blockchain-Powered Payments" | (19)

"Capital One Files Patent For Blockchain-based User Authentication" | (20)

"Banks pour $107M into blockchain consortium R3" | (21)

"CEO of UBS: Blockchain Will Transform Cost Base of Financial Services Industry" | (22)

"Here's Why Bank of America Has Filed Nearly 50 Blockchain-Related Patents" | (23)

"Banking Giants Including Citigroup and Barclays Sign Up for a Trial Blockchain Project" | (24)

"Morgan Stanley Joins Goldman Sachs in Clearing Bitcoin Futures" | (25)

"Morgan Stanley Hires Credit Suisse Crypto Expert as Head of Digital Asset Markets" | (26)

From the headlines, I could see that the "Big" banks were in and other Wall Street financial institutions were on their way.

Every day on Twitter or YouTube, I would hear someone referencing, "The Herd is coming". I listened to a podcast where I learned that as early as October 2017, #RabbitHoleResource - Michael Novogratz, made popular the crypto phrase "The Herd is Coming". Michael Novogratz is an ex-hedge fund manager, formerly of the investment firm Fortress Investment Group. Forbes magazine ranked him as a billionaire in 2007 and 2008 and prior to joining Fortress, he was a partner at Goldman Sachs. (27)

Mr. Novogratz was a speaker at the cryptocurrency conference, Ethereal Summit San Francisco, in 2017, where he titled his presentation "The Herd is Coming", referencing the inevitability of institutional capital. I watched the YouTube clip of his presentation, where he went over how he got into the crypto space, the potential for cryptos and blockchain, and how he felt that the established mainstream institutions would adopt cryptos. He spoke of how the institutional minds and money were looking more and more at bitcoin and cryptos as legitimate and were trying to figure out ways that they could get skin into the game. (28)

All throughout 2018, Novogratz's speculation was backed up by further news headlines that reported on several major institutional giants that were testing out the crypto market. I read one article that reported on Goldman Sachs' plan to open a Bitcoin trading desk. Another article pointed out that Goldman-backed Circle bought Poloniex, a cryptocurrency trading exchange. Listening to the Crypto Sphere Podcast (29), I learned that Barclays bank was interested in starting its own trading desk and that George Soros gave the green light to trade crypto. However, one of the biggest institutional headlines in 2018 that the crypto influencers were talking about was the news about Bakkt's entrance into the market. At the time #RabbitHoleResource - Kelly Loeffler was the CEO of Bakkt. She later would go on to be appointed to the US Senate from Georgia to replace the retiring Johnny Isakson.

Mrs. Loeffler indicated that Bakkt was a joint venture created by the Intercontinental Exchange (ICE). ICE operates 23 stock exchanges including the New York Stock Exchange, which trades over 1.5 billion shares daily, so they are seen as bringing credibility to the crypto space. In addition to ICE, Mrs. Loeffler stated that Bakkt is supported by both Microsoft and Starbucks. The capital backing Bakkt makes it a profoundly serious crypto platform. Mrs. Loeffler announced the launch of Bakkt in an August 2018 Medium article, which outlined a long list of investing partners that included Fortress Investment Group, Eagle Seven, Galaxy Digital, Horizons Ventures, Alan Howard, and Pantera Capital. (30)

The Medium article went on to say that Bakkt is a Bitcoin futures exchange that allows investors to invest in Bitcoin futures, which are particularly interesting to institutional investors. This was especially interesting to Bitcoin maximalist also because Bakkt was introducing the first institutional onramp, which included physically settled bitcoin futures. All the prior bitcoin future products were cash settled instead of bitcoin settled. The availability of physically backed Bitcoin futures was a major advancement for the crypto market. According to industry experts, increasing the availability of complex financial products backed by physical Bitcoin attracts more institutional capital to the crypto market without the negative impact of paper futures on price movements. Expert say that large-scale institutional investors settling Bakkt Bitcoin futures contracts will need to purchase large amounts of Bitcoin. This will inject fiat currency into the cryptocurrency market, increasing the bitcoin market cap and potentially resulting in higher demand and positive price action.

In addition to Bakkt, in 2018 I found out through watching *The Gentlemen of Crypto* YouTube channel that the giant Wall Street firm, Fidelity, spent four to five years reviewing crypto before they launched Fidelity Digital Assets, an institutional platform like Bakkt (31). In an interview with Frank Chaparro, Senior Correspondent at The Block, Tom Jessop, the head of Fidelity Digital Assets, announced that Fidelity, one of the world biggest asset managers (about $2.5 trillion worth of assets under management) has finally entered the cryptocurrency world. The Block report indicated that leading up to the creation and release of the platform, Fidelity said that they interviewed about 450 institutions ranging from wealthy family offices, hedge funds, pensions, and endowments, and received great feedback. Of the 450 interviewed, roughly twenty percent of the respondents indicated that they owned cryptocurrency and planned on doubling their allocations over the next five years. (32) This is a large percentage of institutional clients compared to the percentage of average retail investors that report owning bitcoin, which we saw in the Wells Fargo / Gallop survey was about two percent.

I also learned that the equity trading platform, TD Ameritrade had also jumped into the game by investing in a new cryptocurrency exchange called ErisX in a bid to offer their clients digital asset investment options beyond bitcoin. According to TD Ameritrade's website, ErisX is an innovative company that offers traders access to cryptocurrency spot contracts, as well as futures contracts, on a single exchange. TD Ameritrade told their clients, which I was one of them, that ErisX was a strategic investment, which was yet another way for them to demonstrate their ongoing commitment to innovation, and to bring their clients a best-in-class investing and trading experience. (33) Why are all these traditional brokers getting into crypto? Are they trying to give us clues or are they taking clues from their customer demand?

The next biggest institutional headlines out of 2018 that I was hearing centered on US investment firm VanEck. In June 2018, VanEck joined blockchain software and financial services company SolidX to apply for a physically backed Bitcoin Exchanged Traded Fund (ETF), to be listed on CBOE's Equities Exchange. Remember, an ETF is just a fancy mutual fund. This news drove the crypto community wild. This is what most of us was waiting for; that ETF that Teeka was talking about that would usher in mass adoption by Main Street America.

For more than a year, several investment-management firms had been pushing for a bitcoin exchange-traded fund (ETF), a financial vehicle which would allow retail customers to purchase cryptocurrency through stock brokerage accounts. VanEck's history with traditional ETFs and their reputation as a major investment firm gave everyone in the crypto space confidence that they could convince the Securities and Exchange Commission (SEC) to approve their bitcoin ETF application. However, to our frustration, the US Securities and Exchange Commission has denied or delayed every proposal for a crypto-linked ETF.

To most people in the crypto community, the SEC's hesitation to approve a bitcoin ETF seemed confusing. After all, cryptocurrencies are widely available on other platforms, including US based digital asset exchanges like **#RabbitHoleResource** - Coinbase and Gemini. Crypto proponents say that a bitcoin ETF would make cryptocurrency more widely available to mainstream investors. Furthermore, an ETF would place bitcoin alongside equities in investment portfolios, giving more customers a comprehensive view of their overall assets.

2018 seemed to be the year for institutional adoption. Not to be outdone by the big banks and financial institutions, the Ivy league endowment funds wanted in on the crypto game as well. Reports from Cointelegraph, reported that Harvard, MIT, and Stanford were among several prestigious US universities that have made investments into cryptocurrency funds. They reported that the multi-billion endowments of Harvard University, Stanford University, Dartmouth College, Massachusetts Institute of Technology (MIT), and the University of North Carolina had all invested capital in the crypto space. (34) People on Twitter believed that this was a sign of the asset class' growing acceptance among institutional investors.

All my crypto YouTubers were quoting from a CNBC news article in October of 2018, where David Swensen, who manages Yale University's $29.4 billion endowment, invested in two funds dedicated to cryptocurrencies. They said that the funds are run by **#RabbitHoleResource** - Andreessen Horowitz and Paradigm. David Swensen is widely considered one of the world's top money managers. Although crypto is a tiny allocation in Swensen's nearly $30 billion portfolio, if you add up all the allocations from the other ivy league endowments, you can see that the institutional money coming into crypto is significant. It was reported that in 2018, Harvard University's endowment was around $39.2 billion, making it by far the largest university endowment across the globe. If just the top ten endowments allocated only one percent of their fund to crypto, you can get an idea of the type of money that we suspect is flowing into the space.

The crypto influencer that I listen to the most is **#RabbitHoleResource** - Anthony Pompliano. He goes by Pomp on Twitter and he has a daily newsletter and YouTube channel. Pomp is a partner at Morgan Creek Capital. I also met Pomp at the Blockland Solutions Cleveland crypto conference and interacted with him on Twitter often. Pomp is famous for creating the crypto tag line, "Long bitcoin, short the bankers". Pomp said that two public pension funds are dipping their toes into the world of crypto venture capital and that as far as he knew, no one other than Morgan Creek had raised crypto venture capital from a public pension. (35)

Pomp said that Morgan Creek started a venture fund with $40 million invested. The two public pensions anchoring the fund were Fairfax County, Virginia's Police Officer's Retirement System and Employees' Retirement System. He said that the new fund's investors also include a university endowment, a hospital system, an insurance company, and a private foundation. Pomp indicated that the investors were interested in the crypto fund due to the attractive asymmetric return profile that it represented.

On Pomp's podcast, he indicated that the police pension fund has $1.45 billion in assets, while the fund for Fairfax government employees has $4.25 billion. He further went on to explain that the size of the two funds helps to illuminate the potential of bringing public pensions into blockchain investing. Such entities can take large positions in crypto funds using an exceedingly small portion of their assets under management. Pomp said that the fund has already closed deals in some of the most established names in crypto, including Coinbase, Bakkt, BlockFi, TrustToken, Harbor and Good Money, among others.

As we have seen, 2018 demonstrated that the Herd did come, and they came with a mission. It appears to me that they plan to stay, and they intend to take over the crypto space. This is a new profit frontier for the big money investors.

The entrance of these big players seems to have come with some pros and cons. We talked about the pros being the fact that a lot of the institutional money is being used in the form of venture capital and going to companies and projects that are building the infrastructure to make it easier for institutions and retail investors to enter the crypto market, such as the bitcoin futures and retail equity/crypto exchanges. This will certainly help with further mass adoption of bitcoin and other cryptocurrencies.

On the other hand, we saw that although the big institutional investors could survive the price drop of the severe bear market, many small investors just could not take the volatility and they are being pushed out of the market. Some people went so far as to suggest that the big guys purposely drove the prices down for this and other reasons.

Whatever the case, the result is that throughout my nine months in the crypto space, despite the entrance of new institutional money, new crypto companies, and new crypto products, brought in by the big Wall Street institutional investors, I still fail to see an increase in women or minority faces in this space. The early adopter advantage seems to only be taken advantage by a select group of privileged people and these people do not seem to want to readily share.

Either way, the institutional herd seems to be benefiting from its early adopter advantage. As like Pomp likes to say, it is certainly time for more institutions to "Get off of Zero" and put at least a small allocation of one percent to five percent of their capital into the crypto market. I concur but also say that it is not too late for the small retail investor, especially women and minorities, to do the same. In crypto it only takes a small allocation to make an outsized return.

I am not an Investment Advisor. This is not investment advice.

CHAPTER 3

Facebook vs. Government vs. Bitcoin

The 7 Superpowers of Bitcoin:

#3 – PSEUDONYMOUS

Pseudonymous is bitcoin's power to transact without giving any personally identifying information. People often describe Bitcoin as anonymous. However, achieving reasonable anonymity with bitcoin can be quite complicated and perfect anonymity may be impossible. Instead, bitcoin is Pseudonymous. Satoshi Nakamoto designed Bitcoin to allow its users to send and receive payments with an acceptable level of privacy as well as any other form of money apart from cash. In Bitcoin, your pseudonym is the address to which you receive bitcoin. Every transaction involving that address is stored forever in the blockchain. If your address is ever linked to your identity, every transaction will be linked to you. In the Bitcoin whitepaper, Satoshi recommended that bitcoin users use a new address for each transaction to avoid the transactions being linked to a common owner.

Today is July 14, 2019. The price for a full bitcoin is $10,256.06 and bitcoin's market cap is $182.7B. We are still early. Bitcoin still not dead.

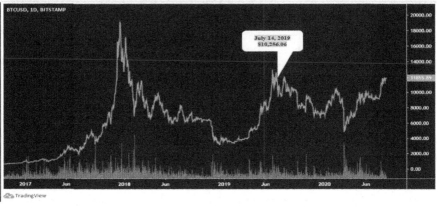

(1)

I still consider myself a newbie, but it has been about sixteen months since I stepped into the crypto space. Bitcoin is ten and a half years old and everyday it survives, makes it that much stronger. The techies call that the Lindy Effect, which states that the life expectancy of a technology is proportional to its current age, so that every additional period of survival implies a longer remaining life expectancy. (36) In short, Bitcoiners just say, "The longer Bitcoin survives, the harder it is to kill it".

Right now, it is feeling good to be a Bitcoiner. Bitcoin has gone above the phycological price barrier of $10K. At the current price of $10,256.06, bitcoin is up over 250% since the lows of December 2018. These are the asymmetrical gains that traders like to see in bitcoin. Traders are feeling good about bitcoin now. However, as a HODLer, I really do not care what the price is now because I am not selling any time soon, but it does feel good as the price continues to rise.

July 14th is a special day for me. It is my wife's (fiancé at the time) birthday, so we are celebrating down in South Florida on Singer Island with friends and family. Fun is had by all. My crypto portfolio is looking good and I am in a good mood, so I rented a convertible and hit the highways of South Florida. We spent some quality time on the beaches of Fort Lauderdale and down on Miami South Beach. This was a great birthday weekend. Life is good, but is it? Well yes it was, but something was brewing in the crypto world.

On July 15, 2019, Facebook announced that its cryptocurrency will not launch until all regulatory concerns have been met and it has all the appropriate approvals. Wait! What? Facebook is launching a cryptocurrency! Well a month earlier, on June 18, 2019, Facebook formally announced its intention to launch its own cryptocurrency called Libra. (37)Facebook was ready to enter the financial services industry and challenge the financial status quo and I was fully behind them in this effort. However, there were mixed opinions about this in the crypto community. There were endless tweet storms and Medium posts about this big news.

The crypto news site CCN, published an article called, "21 Brutally Honest Opinions About Facebook's Libra Cryptocurrency", where they captured some opinions from the Bitcoin community. Here are my top five responses:

#**RabbitHoleResource** -

1. Ryan Selkis (Messari CEO) – Facebook's Libra is a *"gateway drug" for crypto.*
2. Andreas Antonopoulos (Bitcoin evangelist and educator) -- *"Is Facebook's Libra a real blockchain? No. Will it compete against Bitcoin and truly open, public blockchains? Never."*
3. Nic Carter (Castle Island Ventures) -- *"If Facebook can pull off this ambitious scheme, it accelerates the inevitable collapse of the long tail of sovereign currencies."*
4. Changpeng Zhao (Binance CEO) -- *"Facebook should accept bitcoin (and BNB of course) alone side [sic] Libra in the WhatsApp, Messenger, Facebook, and Instagram apps."*
5. Cameron Winklevoss -- *"Prediction: every FAANG company will have its own coin within 24 months."*

(38)

I had to go to the Libra whitepaper to see just what Facebook wanted to accomplish with their Libra project, which they wanted to launch in 2020. Right away I am thinking that this is a genius idea. Facebook has over two billion customers already. This is a perfect way to usher in mass adoption of digital assets. I hoped that they would just utilize bitcoin on their platforms, but if they must create their own cryptocurrency then, so be it. It will still encourage interest and participation in the overall crypto space in my opinion. This could truly be the first global currency the world has ever utilized on a massive scale if Facebook gets what they want.

After I read the Libra whitepaper, I printed and kept a copy because I think in the future this may well prove to be a historical document. I keep it nice and safe next to my copy of the Bitcoin whitepaper. If I ever meet Mark Z, I am going to ask him to autograph it. From the Libra whitepaper, I could tell that Facebook's aim was global, not only were they going to go after their existing two billion customer base, but they were targeting the population of two billion unbanked and underbanked people worldwide. Facebook wanted to make it as easy and affordable to move money around the world as it is to send a text message.

If you remember, about a year ago, I was warning my senior management at the bank that crypto was coming for the bank's customers. The bank still has no response. With cryptocurrencies like bitcoin and Libra, as long as you have a cell phone, a computer, and/or an internet connection, you can digitally access and transact with your money with lower fees and 24/7/365 uptime because unlike the 9:00 – 5:00 traditional banking hours, the crypto market does not close or take off for weekends and holidays. You have access to your money anytime you need it. I take advantage of this every week. Every Sunday evening, I purchase a little bit of bitcoin through the **#RabbitHoleResource** - Cash App **#StackingSatsSunday**, then I immediately send a portion to my personal Ledger cryptocurrency hardware wallet and the rest to **#RabbitHoleResource** - BlockFi, where I earn over five percent interest compounded every month. Even my employee bank account at the bank cannot compete with that rate. Crypto banking products are just all around better than traditional banking products. I can manage all this money movement on a weekend, after hours, in less than twenty minutes. I do not have to wait for the traditional weekday business hours or the traditional three-day settlement time to move or spend my money. In crypto, everything is near instant.

Digital asset benefits such as these are attractive well beyond the US population. That is why Facebook is targeting populations in Africa, Southeast Asia, and Latin America, where Libra will serve as a superior form of payment and wealth preservation.

According to Libra's whitepaper, the Libra project has received financial backing from around twenty-five Founding Member companies including eBay, Uber, Lyft, Spotify, Visa, Mastercard, PayPal, Coinbase, and venture capital firm Andreessen Horovitz. Facebook says that they are trying to attract one hundred Founding Member companies before they launch. (39)

You would think that there is no stopping this social media giant, with backing from some of the most innovative companies in business, but not so fast, the US government has not had its say, and unfortunately, it is unlikely that the government wants any changes to the financial status quo that Facebook is trying to challenge.

I thought that I had a busy July with planning my wife's birthday trip to Florida, but that was nothing compared to what the US government was busy doing. All throughout July of 2019, the government was planning and plotting their response to Facebook's surprise cryptocurrency announcement. The US government probably had the most severe criticism out of all the interested parties around the world who were shocked by Facebook's announcement.

The US government officials wasted no time responding, trying to get out in front of what they perceived as serious privacy, trading, national security, and monetary policy concerns. Let me interpret that for you. They perceived Libra as a threat to the US dollar and in turn a threat to US power and standing in the world.

On July 2, **#BlackExcellence - ** Congresswoman Maxine Waters (Auntie Maxine as we like to call her in the Black community), Chairwoman of the House Financial Services Committee, wrote a direct letter to Facebook's CEO, Mark Zuckerberg, requesting an immediate moratorium on the implementation of Facebook's proposed cryptocurrency. Auntie Maxine was not shy, she wanted the world to know that the US government will defend its precious US dollar. She posted the full letter on the government's website. The letter read in part,

> *"Because Facebook is already in the hands of over a quarter of the world's population, it is imperative that Facebook and its partners immediately cease implementation plans until regulators and Congress have an opportunity to examine these issues and take action... During this moratorium, we intend to hold public hearings on the risks and benefits of cryptocurrency-based activities and explore legislative solutions. Failure to cease implementation before we can do so, risks a new Swiss-based financial system that is too big to fail." - (40)*

Wow! Auntie don't play that! She don't care about no Libra or no "Bit-Corn"! I joke a bit because Chairwoman Walters was taped on a CNBC television clip mistakenly referring to bitcoin as Bit-Corn. The crypto community got a kick out of that and used it as a meme referring to older people who never heard of and do not understand bitcoin.

I love Auntie Maxine. I consider her one of the most powerful Black women in the United States. She is a very accomplished Congress woman. However, I totally disagree with her initial stance toward Bitcoin and cryptocurrency. She is certainly an ally the Bitcoin community needs on its side. I realize that her current stance comes from her total unawareness and I believe that the Congressional hearings into Libra will help shed light on cryptocurrency to an older Congressional audience. But what Chairwomen Walters fails to realize is that certain crypto projects, specifically Bitcoin and any other decentralized projects, are going to advance whether she wants them to or not. That is the beauty of decentralization. Crypto-currency is a global issue now and the race has certainly begun in countries around the world. Countries like China and Russia are not waiting. They are either going to position their countries into Bitcoin, a decentralized cryptocurrency that cannot be controlled by a central government, or they are going to create their own. My guess is that these countries are going to do both over time.

Bitcoin and cryptocurrency cross all political parties. I am calling on Chairwoman Walters to listen to the more progressive voices on the House Financial Services Committee like Republican Congressman Warren Davidson who serves Ohio's 8th Congressional District. Davidson is educated and is a proponent of the US using crypto-currency and blockchain technology as a competitive advantage in global affairs. I first came across Representative Davidson because he was a speaker at the first Blockland Solutions Cleveland cryptocurrency conference. Congressman Davidson co-sponsored a bipartisan bill in Congress with Democratic Congressman Darren Soto called the Token Taxonomy Act, to update the US laws on cryptocurrencies. Davidson and Soto believe that light tough regulation is needed to give US companies and entrepreneurs the certainty they need to foster innovation and create jobs.

I am also calling on Congresswoman Alexandria Ocasio-Cortez, better known as AOC, who is also on the House Financial Services Committee to support Davidson and Soto. AOC is a Democratic Congresswoman serving as the US Representative for New York's 14th congressional district.

Taking office at age 29, Ocasio-Cortez is the youngest woman ever to serve in the United States Congress. I take note of her because of her substantial Twitter presence. As a young, powerful, person of color, her advocacy grabbed my attention. She advocates a progressive platform that includes Medicare for All, a federal jobs guarantee, the Green New Deal, abolishing the US Immigration and Customs Enforcement, free public college and trade school, and a seventy percent marginal tax rate on millionaire fortunes. AOC is a young fresh voice in Congress and the crypto community would benefit greatly from her advocacy of this digital finance issue.

On July 10th, the US Federal Reserve Charmain, Jerome Powell weighed in. During his semi-annual testimony on monetary policy before Chairwoman Walters' Financial Services Committee, Jerome said,

> *"Libra raises many serious concerns regarding privacy, money laundering, consumer protection and financial stability.... I*

don't think the project can go forward without addressing those concerns…Facebook has a couple billion-plus users, so I think you have for the first time the possibility of very broad adoption of cryptocurrency." - (41)

Seems Mr. Powell and I both had the same idea on how Libra could affect mass adoption of crypto.

On July 12th, the President of the United States, Donald Trump took to Twitter and added his two cents,

"Facebook Libra's 'virtual currency' will have little standing or dependability. If Facebook and other companies want to become a bank, they must seek a new Banking Charter and become subject to all Banking Regulations, just like other Banks…I am not a fan of Bitcoin and other Cryptocurrencies, which are not money, and whose value is highly volatile and based on thin air…Unregulated Crypto Assets can facilitate unlawful behavior, including drug trade and other illegal activity." - (42)

That is funny. That sounds like the US dollar.

On July 16th, the US Senate Banking Committee held hearings on Libra and on July 17th, the House Financial Services Committee held hearings on Libra. While I was celebrating and relaxing in Florida, the US government was launching an assault against Mark Zuckerberg and Facebook over crypto. The US government was finally waking up to the disruptive innovation of crypto started by Bitcoin. You could sense the fear in the air. It took Facebook, to open the eyes of the world to the power of digital assets.

The Bitcoin Maximalist community just sat back and smiled to ourselves. This was the beauty of Bitcoin. It is an opensource software program not controlled by any centralized authority. It does not have a CEO that Congress can bring in front of any committee to grill and say stop your project. The Bitcoin network is over ten years old and its untouchable. Bitcoin continues to quietly mine blocks in its blockchain, day after day, and allows its users to do with their money as they see fit, no matter what Auntie or anyone else has to say about it.

Within a year, the government went from ignore it, to shut it down, to we want in! You know the old saying, "If you can't beat them, join them." It appears that the US government learned a lot from the Congressional hearings it had with Facebook executives. They came to know the benefits of digital currencies that I spoke about, more efficient; safer; less expensive; faster; and more accessible. Any smart businessperson presented with these facts have no other choice but to consider competitive options.

After the Congressional hearings, a few Congressmen wrote a letter to the Chairman of the US Federal Reserve, Jerome Powell, asking whether the central bank had investigated the potential of a central bank digital currency (CBDC). The Fed Chair confirmed that the Federal Reserve was considering several options.

On October 16, 2019, Fed Governor, Lael Brainard gave a speech entitled "Digital Currencies, Stablecoins, and the Evolution of Payments Landscape" at a banking conference called The Future of Money in the Digital Age. She said,

> "The Facebook Libra project imparted urgency to the conversation around digital currencies. We are collaborating with other central banks as we advance our understanding of central bank digital currencies."

She went on to say,

> "The prospect for rapid adoption of global stablecoin payment systems has intensified calls for central banks to issue digital currencies in order to maintain the sovereign currency as the anchor of the nation's payment systems."- (43)

As always in the financial innovation space, it appears that the US government is playing catch up. It had been rumors in the crypto community for months that countries such as China and Russia had already been researching and preparing to launch their nation's Central Bank Digital Currency (CBDC).

All the governments around the world are beginning to realize that technology will usher in a cashless society eventually. Countries such as Sweden, China, and the United Kingdom, are virtually there now (44). However, all governments now are realizing that a central bank digital currency could serve as the backbone for a new, secure, real-time payment and settlement system. They are now realizing if they do not create their own digital currency, the world will gravitate to the best digital currency and that is bitcoin.

I feel that this will be the ultimate outcome over the next twenty years even if the government puts in place their own currency because bitcoin will always have a superior monetary policy. The CBDC will still have the same flawed monetary policy as its fiat cash, just in a digital format. The government will still be able to print as much money as they want, out of thin air, and debase the currency through inflation like they currently do by policy.

If you have humans as your centralized authority controlling your monetary policy, you are always going to be subject to the possibility of corruption or incompetence. More and more, our society is choosing to trust computer code and algorithms over human based decisions. These days I rely on Google Maps more than asking the person out of the window for directions. Amazon knows what I want to watch on TV and what I want to buy from the store better than I do and this is due to technology algorithms. Soon everyone will realize that it only makes sense to trust the software program of Bitcoin over the whims of central bankers who are in control of the monetary policy and decisions of centralized monetary currencies.

(45)

Would you trust these people in this photo to decide your monetary future?

This was a photo that the European Central Bank (ECB) Chairwoman, Christine Lagarde posted on Twitter and it immediately became one of the best crypto memes of the year.

On November 14, 2019, Lagarde tweeted,

> *"I was pleased to invite my new Governing Council colleagues to join me at an off-site retreat yesterday. We discussed in an open and informal setting the running of the Governing Council."* (45)

There is an example of some true diversity, equity, and inclusion going on in that room, NOT.

It is funny because you can barely notice that she is in the photo. Although she is the President, she is the only woman on the council and not one minority face to be seen. Lagarde had just taken office two weeks before this photo. In the picture you have the twenty-five members of the ECB's Governing Council who gathered for a retreat in a nineteenth-century castle outside of Frankfurt, Germany to discuss Europe's monetary policy and no doubt, cryptocurrency was probably on the agenda.

According to Christine Lagarde's LinkedIn bio, on July 2011 Christine Lagarde became the eleventh Managing Director of the International Monetary Fund (IMF), and the first woman to hold that position. She launched a wide-ranging work agenda on the reform of the international monetary system. In 2018, she was ranked the third most influential woman in the world by Forbes magazine. She resigned from the IMF on September 12, 2019 following her nomination as President of the European Central Bank and she went on to take up her role as ECB President on November 1, 2019. (46)

People in the Ripple (XRP) cryptocurrency community love Christine Lagarde because when she was the Managing Director of the International Monetary Fund (IMF), she would always praise crypto and the idea of using digital assets in the international money settlement space that Ripple and XRP are trying to disrupt. When she became President of the ECB, the XRP community had high hopes that she would steer Europe into the crypto direction. This is one reason I am holding my bag of XRP, just in case.

That photo and subsequent meme of Chairwoman Lagarde and the ECB Governing council inspired me to write this book. Do I trust that group of people to create diverse and inclusive policies that would be good for people like me? No, I do not. The US Federal Reserve central bank is not much better in their diversity and inclusion. Bitcoin fixes this all around the world. This is an example of why I say that it is imperative for women and minorities to join the crypto movement. Crypto is currently mirroring the traditional financial system but I do not want to see the crypto space continue to be a monolithic environment where only the wealthy and privileged benefit. This could have detrimental effects in an economic crisis. For instance, the current events, which are playing out, are proving just how detrimental an economic crisis can be and how valuable bitcoin is in a crisis.

There is no denying it now, it is here! For weeks it has been "Their" problem overseas, but not anymore. Today is Monday, March 23, 2020 and I am already seven days into my own shelter in place quarantine. Yesterday, following disturbing data from the Center of Disease Control (CDC), the Governor of Ohio signed an order directing all Ohioans to stay at home and maintain social distancing of at least six feet from each other until further notice due to the world-wide pandemic spread of the novel Corona Virus Disease 2019 (COVID-19).

No, this is not the introduction to a science fiction story. This is occurring state by state throughout the United States. Ohio is just the seventh state to make the stay at home order mandatory. They have closed all schools, restaurant dining rooms, bars, bowling alleys, barbershops, nail salons, and all non-essential businesses, effectively grinding the economy to a halt. On top of that, in the last two weeks, the US stock market crashed over thirty percent, to lows that have not been seen since 2016.

The United States' reaction to this health crisis has caused another economic crisis. Unlike the economic crisis caused by the banks in 2008, the economic crisis of 2020 seems worse. More than 30 million Americans to date have filed for unemployment and thousands of businesses have closed their doors for good and as the economic conditions continued to worsen, millions more people continued to file for unemployment each week.

However, the US Congress did not sit back idle. They knew the economic situation was a disaster, so they quickly passed legislation that would inject liquidity into the economy. The legislation included various lending programs, asset purchases, and monetary stimulus packages directly aimed at helping businesses and individuals. The initial stimulus package was approximately $2 trillion. However, as time continued and the situation worsened, Congress felt that we needed another $3 trillion of monetary stimulus to continue fighting the economic impact. Economists call this monetary stimulus quantitative easing or QE for short.

Investopedia defines quantitative easing as,

> *"a form of unconventional monetary policy in which a central bank purchases longer-term securities from the open market in order to increase the money supply and encourage lending and investment. Buying these securities adds new money to the economy, and also serves to lower interest rates by bidding up fixed-income securities. It also greatly expands the central bank's balance sheet."* (47)

My favorite description of QE comes from Crypto Twitter. "Printer go Brrrr" is a meme going through Crypto Twitter. It refers to the sound of continuous money printing by the US Federal Reserve.

It's unfortunate but, central banks, such as the US Federal Reserve, only have two tools at their disposal to combat an economic crisis, 1) Adjust interest rates, and 2) print money (QE) and leading into this crisis the Federal Reserve has already cut interest rates to zero percent.

We are living in ironic times. This economic crisis is giving the world a lesson in monetary policy 101. The average citizen is seeing the Federal Reserve print trillions of dollars, which is likely to lead to hyperinflation and a loss of confidence in the US dollar over a long period of time. The US government is creating money out of thin air, which of course will also increase our national debt level. It looks like our national debt deficit could be more than $5 trillion, an almost twenty-five percent increase in the national debt in a single year.

To the average joe, all this money printing feels good in our pocket in the short term. They just sent me and every adult American $1,200 of free money in hopes that we will spend it and stimulate the economy. Most Bitcoiners say that they used it to buy bitcoin. There is actually a Twitter account that tracks how much the $1,200 stimulus check is worth if you invested it in bitcoin. The Congress and the Federal Reserve was trying to come up with a quick way to implement their central bank digital currency (CBDC) so that they could easily give everyone a digital wallet connected directly to the Federal Reserve Bank and deposit every American a digital payment. However, they did not have enough time to implement that plan. Therefore, they just did ACH direct deposits through the IRS for some and sent paper checks to others. However, in the long term, our next generations are going to feel the pain. It is simply impossible to print trillions of dollars and not see inflation over the long term. That inflation will drive the wealth inequality gap to the largest disparity that it has ever been. The large population of Americans who live paycheck to paycheck and cannot afford a $1,000 emergency expense, will see their wealth eaten away by inflation.

This is not unique to the United States. Every government that has a fiat currency has the same structural issue. Their currencies are all backed by the full faith of the government instead of by an underlying commodity such as gold, like it used to be in the world before 1971. This was called the Gold Standard. These current fiat currencies are slowly debased away through inflation. A small group of people within the government (central bankers), controls the rate of debasement and the citizens of a country are generally required to trust this group of people with the sustainability and value of their currency.

What most people do not realize is that inflation reduces the value of cash, however it increases the value of other assets. Rich people love this because they hold lots of other assets and do not keep much of their wealth in cash. On the other hand, the average Main Street citizen does not own any stock. They do not own any real estate. They own no gold or bonds either. They simply live paycheck-to-paycheck and do not own many non-cash assets. This is why we hear the phrase, "the rich get richer and the poor get poorer". This has been going on for decades and the wealth inequality gap has only widened.

Speaking of rich people, Paul Tudor Jones, a famous billionaire hedge fund manager, recently disclosed that he is buying bitcoin. He was quoted as saying,

> *"The best profit-maximizing strategy is to own the fastest horse. If I am forced to forecast, my bet is it will be Bitcoin."* (48)

He said that he was gaining exposure to Bitcoin as a hedge against the coming inflation.

This is a good time to lightly touch on Bitcoin's economic monetary policy properties. First, Bitcoin demonstrates the concept of quantitative hardening (QH). The idea of quantitative hardening is the exact opposite of quantitative easing (QE). QE injects liquidity into a market by increasing the monetary supply and decreasing the value of each individual unit of that currency. Quantitative Hardening (QH) drops the liquidity being injected into a market by decreasing the incoming daily supply and it increases the value of each individual unit of that currency. The Bitcoin algorithm creates and injects a pre-set amount of Bitcoin into the circulating supply approximately every ten minutes. This is done programmatically and is not controlled by anyone. It started at fifty Bitcoin per ten minutes and continued to execute that flawlessly for four years. At that point, the fifty Bitcoin was cut in half to twenty-five Bitcoin, where it remained for the next four years. We then saw a programmatic cut to 12.5 Bitcoin every ten minutes, then a cut to 6.25 bitcoin, which is where we are today. Each of these cuts in incoming daily supply is known as the Bitcoin halving. This event creates quantitative hardening by definition. (35)

The second property of Bitcoin's economic monetary policy is that Bitcoin is designed with an artificially capped supply. There will only ever be twenty-one million Bitcoin created. Each time one is lost or destroyed; they are gone forever. This makes the macro design of Bitcoin deflationary. We cannot create more of them, but we can see a total supply reduction over time.

Property number three is that Bitcoin is a non-correlated asymmetric asset. Non-correlated refers to the fact that bitcoin historical price movement does not follow any other asset class. Growth or decline in stocks, commodities or gold does not correlate to a rise or fall in bitcoin price. Asymmetric typically refers to the risk/reward returns of an asset. Put simply, Bitcoin has much more upside potential than downside. Bitcoin could gain 10,000% in the absolute bull case or it could lose one hundred percent in worst bear case.

Finally, Bitcoin is just a better form of sound, hard money. This is why many governments around the world are looking at tokenizing all the fiat currencies. As we can see from the Fed statements, there will be a digital dollar. A digital euro. A digital yuan. And so on and so on.

More and more people and institutions are realizing that bitcoin is like digital gold and serves as a hedge against inflation. The problem is that those who are realizing and taking advantage of this fact are more so the savvy Wall Street investors and they are coming into the space in droves. However, the average Main Street investors, such as I, are only trickling into the Bitcoin space one by one.

CHAPTER 4

Key #1 – Learn Bitcoin

The 7 Superpowers of Bitcoin:

#4 – CENSORSHIP RESISTANT

Censorship Resistance is Bitcoin's power that demonstrates the idea that no nation-state, corporation, or third party has the power to control who you can receive value from, send value to, or where you can store your wealth on the network as long as you follow the rules of the network protocol. Censorship-resistance ensures that the laws that govern the network are set in advance and cannot be retroactively altered to fit a specific agenda.

Today is October 12, 2019. The price for a full bitcoin is $8,336.56 and bitcoin's market cap is $150.0B. We are still early. Bitcoin still not dead.

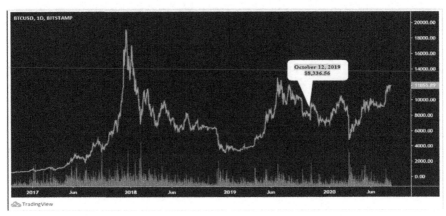

(1)

I cannot believe it. Thirty years ago, today, I became a father for the very first time to a beautiful baby girl we named Asia. I was only twenty-one years old, still in college, and had no idea what the future would bring. However, as I look back, that was one of my happiest days on Earth, one that would alter the course for the rest of my life.

Becoming a father opened my eyes to becoming a responsible adult. One of the first things new parents think about is keeping your child safe and providing a secure financial future for them. That is exactly what her mother and I planned to do as parents. A few years after I got out of college, I got into the financial services industry as a Registered Rep for a major securities firm. This is where I began to develop my financial literacy. The things that I was learning about economics, wealth, and money in the real world, I wondered why I had never been taught these principles in high school or even in college. I was just a young man selling complex financial products to older wealthy people that only one year prior, I had no idea these financial products existed. To make it worse, I was selling some products that I could not even purchase myself because I was not an accredited investor. To buy these types of investments you had to have investable assets over $1 million or earn over $250,000 per year. So basically, these financial products were only for the rich. Yes, I was able to set up whole life insurance policies and traditional annuities, and college education plans, for my family, but I was not able to get into ground floor start up investments, or private equity deals that the wealthy investors had access to. It did not matter how financially literate I was about these products, if you did not have money, you could not make money with these investments. The only test you had was your bank account.

This was my first exposure to the fact that there is a totally different game on Wall Street than there is on Main Street and that the key to navigating this game is to recognize the fact that the game exists, then learning the rules and how to play the game. The alternative to that is to create your own game. That is what Bitcoin did when Satoshi Nakamoto published the Bitcoin whitepaper on October 31, 2008. It provided an alternative financial game that would allow anyone to participate.

If January 3, 2019 is Bitcoin's birthday, I consider October 31, 2008 as Bitcoin's conception date. I remember the fall of 2008 vividly. My baby girl was starting her freshman year of college at the University of North Carolina at Chapel Hill. Halloween is famous on many college campuses as being the date for the best parties of the year. UNC Chapel Hill was no different. While my daughter was enjoying her first college Halloween party, Satoshi drops his whitepaper and the era of Bitcoin began.

Now, eleven years after the conception of the Bitcoin whitepaper, my daughter has two children of her own and she is celebrating her thirtieth birthday in Jamaica at an exclusive villa with several of her best girlfriends. These thirty-something Black females are one of my exact target audiences for this book. They all have gone eleven years since the Bitcoin whitepaper and none of them are any wiser about this revolutionary financial technology. For eleven years, Bitcoin has quietly gone along under the radar of most women and minority groups in the United States. But it appears that today these Black women are doing fine for now. They are in Jamaica while I am stuck in Cleveland living vicariously through pictures. I digress. But guess what I got my daughter for her thirtieth birthday, hint, it was bitcoin. This is such a milestone worthy of celebrating. It seems like it was just yesterday when her mother and I were taking her home from the hospital. The older you get; the faster times seems to pass. That is why I know that now more than ever, it is the time to prepare for the next twenty years because before you know it, those two grandchildren of mine will be young adults in a world we will barley recognize today. Fortunately for them, they will grow up in a world that has Bitcoin established as an alternative financial option and hopefully by the time they enter their freshman year of college, they will no longer be considered as underrepresented in the financial economy because now we all have access to this ground floor investment. We are still early.

However, preparation begins with education. In this case I am referring to Bitcoin, crypto, and traditional financial education. I cannot believe that in the twenty-first century, high school and college students are still not receiving the type of education about money that would properly prepare them to thrive in today's world economy. This is why I strongly believe that there is an immediate need to provide a Bitcoin and crypto introduction along with a twenty-first century digital business, finance, and technology education to other average Main Street citizens, specifically, the current and incoming generations of new women and minority investors who have been historically left behind in the traditional financial markets.

For many people like myself in the Bitcoin community, we are looking for the best way to invite people into Bitcoin and make it inclusive and accessible. We believe that Bitcoin needs to be accessible by the common consumer.

After being on my crypto journey for over nineteen months I must admit that crypto and Bitcoin can have a big learning curve depending on how deep you want to travel down the rabbit hole. However, I find that there are three types of people who are not already into Bitcoin.

The first group of people are just people who have never heard of crypto currency and just are not aware of Bitcoin. We are still not mainstream, so we are still early.

The second group of people who are not in Bitcoin yet are the people who are aware of it, but believe it is a scam or that it is worthless. These are people like leaders in the traditional financial markets or people who benefit from companies in the traditional financial markets like Warren Buffet. Warren once called Bitcoin "rat poison squared". Although, Mr. Buffet is a great value investor, he even agrees that he missed the mark on high growth technology investments. Warren also does not like precious metals like silver and gold, so take that for what it is worth.

The third type of person who is not in Bitcoin yet are those people who are aware of it, but they feel that it is too complex or difficult to understand.

I believe that people like me in the Bitcoin community who want to encourage mass adoption of Bitcoin should concentrate on the first and third groups of people that are not currently in Bitcoin. These are the groups that we will have the best chance to educate. The other group will eventually come around on their own. I believe that many of them are probably secretly in Bitcoin anyway.

I found that **#BlackExcellence** – LA Chargers offensive tackle, Russell Okung is a person in the Bitcoin community like me who wants to educate and encourage mass adoption of Bitcoin. Okung made his very public entrance into the Bitcoin community through his tweet that said, "Pay me in bitcoin" on May 13, 2019, which immediately got the attention of Bitcoin Twitter. (49) Since his entrance into the Bitcoin community, Okung has made Bitcoin a topic of conversation on both social media and within the NFL. He even launched his own events brand "Bitcoin Is _". On his website, it says that the mission of "Bitcoin is_" is mainstream adoption. He has an educational platform called Monday Night Bitcoin, a play on Monday Night Football.

In an interview with The Daily HODL, Russel said,

> *"This isn't an event, it's not a conference, it's not a Meetup. This is a revival, man! Bitcoin feels like a renaissance, the great awakening or enlightenment, and that's what we're trying to capture. There's a lot of stuff we can do with Bitcoin Is__ and it's getting a lot of*

transactions. People want to be a part of it. The events we do will be this collision of culture and influence and entertainment and finance and economics. Because Bitcoin is for everyone." (50)

But like I mentioned, educating people on Bitcoin is not an easy job. In early 2020 we had a real-life example play out in the Bitcoin Twitter community where we saw a request for Bitcoin education go terribly wrong, proving how hard Bitcoin is to explain to the average person.

Everyone knows the world renown author, J.K. Rowling. She is the author of the popular book series, *Harry Potter*. J.K. Rowling has 14.5 million Twitter followers. One day J.K. Rowling casually strolled into the Bitcoin Twitter community and asked, "Tell me about Bitcoin". Are you kidding? this is such an opportunity, is what I was thinking. Someone from the mainstream popular culture wants to know more about Bitcoin. Well, what ensued was that she received thousands of technical responses from the Bitcoin Twitter community to which she replied, "I just don't understand what you are telling me." (51) After that, the conversation went terribly left. J.K. Rowling said that she felt attacked by the Bitcoin Twitter community. We missed out on a valuable niche of new adopters. The sci-fi genre is often referred to as "Nerds" just as the Bitcoin and crypto crowds are as well. This was 14.5 million Twitter followers that may be lost forever due to an invitation to Bitcoin education gone wrong.

I did not jump in on the J.K. Rowling Twitter discussion because it quite frankly went away as fast as it came. However, I took that situation as a learning experience. That episode happened while I was in the middle of writing this book. I knew more than ever that this book would be timely and desperately needed in the public as soon as possible. I knew that if my book had been available during the Twitter episode, she could have used my book for answers and to find other suitable educational resources that met her curiosity about Bitcoin.

For example, when I was acquiring my education, I found that there were some mainstream crypto sources that offered user friendly

Bitcoin and crypto education. A few of the large cryptocurrency exchanges included educational pieces on their platforms. For example, #**RabbitHoleResource** - Coinbase Exchange has Coinbase Earn and Coinbase Learn. Coinbase Learn is a set of interactive flashcards for those who want to cover the basics of cryptocurrency, from buying and selling to mining. I believe it is a great resource to share with absolute beginners who have little time and want to get up to speed fast.

Coinbase also has Coinbase Earn. Coinbase offers introductory courses and quizzes in cryptocurrencies that do not have a dedicated course on Coinbase Learn. With these courses and quizzes, you can earn crypto for learning. This allow any learner to get a more holistic view of altcoins and different cryptocurrencies other than the standard courses, which are focused on Bitcoin and Ethereum. You earn small amounts of cryptocurrency for answering quiz questions on a topic so that you will have a small amount to work with for real life application. I took all the quizzes then immediately traded what I earned into bitcoin. But that is just me. I like to stack my satoshis.

The #**RabbitHoleResource** - Gemini crypto exchange has a good beginners education section also called Learn Crypto. They tout it as your go-to crypto resource. They cover:

- What is Bitcoin?
- How Do I Securely Store Bitcoin?
- How Do I Invest in and Trade Bitcoin?
- How Can I Buy Bitcoin?
- What is Bitcoin in 5 minutes?
- What is Orchid in 5 minutes?
- Intro to Crypto Webinar

They have an A-Z crypto glossary that covers everything from Addresses to Zcash.

The cryptocurrency exchange Binance also launched an academy to accelerate crypto and blockchain education. They structured #**RabbitHoleResource** - Binance Academy as an open source platform that is open to both consumers and producers of content.

Besides Binance Academy's in-house content, they welcome submissions of community content. They are positioned as a one-stop-shop for relevant educational articles and videos. Similar to Gemini, Binance Academy also has an A-Z glossary as a companion to navigate through the memes and slang of the crypto community.

However, over my two years of intense crypto engagement I preferred to learn directly from the experts. That is why I stay engaged with my crypto YouTubers and crypto podcasters. Out of hundreds of hours of expert interviews, I would recommend those who are new to the Bitcoin and crypto space to listen to **#RabbitHoleResource** - a seventeen-part beginners guide created by Peter McCormack. Peter hosts the podcast, "What Bitcoin Did".

At the beginning of 2020, Peter created "The Beginner's Guide to Bitcoin" series. He interviewed some of the most well-respected sources in the crypto community. I was able to fill in gaps in my knowledge and bring everything together that I had learned over the two years by listening to his beginner's guide.

The Beginner's Guide to Bitcoin included the following episodes:

- Part 1: Why We Need Bitcoin with Andreas M. Antonopoulos
- Part 2: What Is Money with Parker Lewis
- Part 3: Bitcoin's Pre-History and the Cypherpunks with Aaron van Wirdum
- Part 4: What is Bitcoin with Stephan Livera
- Part 5: The History of Bitcoin with Marty Bent
- Part 6: How Bitcoin Works with Shinobi
- Part 7: Bitcoin's Monetary Policy with Dan Held
- Part 8: How is Bitcoin Legal with Peter Van Valkenburgh & Jerry Brito
- Part 9: Altcoins, A History of Failure with Nic Carter
- Part 10: Buying, Spending and Earning Bitcoin with Matt Odell
- Part 11: Bitcoin and the Macroeconomy with Travis Kling
- Part 12: Bitcoin Privacy & OpSec with Jameson Lopp
- Part 13: The Lightning Network with Jack Mallers
- Part 14: Bitcoin Things You Need to Know with Peter McCormack
- Part 15: Bitcoin FUD with Nic Carter
- Part 16: The Future of Bitcoin with Jeremy Welch
- Part 17: Fuck You, Bitcoin! with John Carvalho

(52)

This was a lot of hours of listening but very well worth it to get a well-rounded education in Bitcoin straight from some of the foremost experts.

When I hear from any successful businessperson or entrepreneur, the overwhelming majority point to Napoleon Hill's original 1937 book *Think & Grow Rich,* as a major tool that guided their financial education to the traditional financial economy. This book has sold over seventy million copies. However, the second and more contemporary book businesspeople point to is Robert Kiyosaki's book *Rich Dad, Poor Dad.* Kiyosaki's book has sold over 32 million copies since 1997. This book teaches the importance of financial literacy, financial independence and building wealth through various methods, such as investing in real estate and owning your own business. If I knew what I know now, I probably would have saved the money I spent on college education for me and my three kids. I could have just settled for two $30 books and I would have been fine.

And what do you know, one of the most renown authors on money and finance is also a Bitcoiner. **#RabbitHoleResource** - Robert Kiyosaki has over 1.3 million Twitter followers. I follow him on Twitter. In 2020, he took to Twitter several times to proclaim his bullish position on Bitcoin. He predicted that by 2023, bitcoin's price would be at least $75,000. Kiyosaki believe that the US dollar and economy are slowly dying, and he believes that gold, silver, and bitcoin are good hedges for what is to come. Kiyosaki says that gold and silver are God's money and bitcoin is open-source people's money.

Robert Kiyosaki tweeted,

(53)

Similar to how people point to Robert Kiyosaki as inspiration in traditional finance education, in the Bitcoin world people often point to **#RabbitHoleResource** - Andreas Antonopoulos. As I listened to several podcast interviews of entrepreneurs in the Bitcoin space, many of them pointed to Andreas or his book *Mastering Bitcoin* as their formal introduction to Bitcoin education.

By October of 2019, I was nineteen months into my crypto journey, and I was trying to round out my crypto education. I was soaking in everything I listened to through crypto YouTube and gaining a lot of knowledge through the podcast interviews I listened to. However, I wanted to test my knowledge not only just to have knowledge, but I wanted to know that I could apply the knowledge and share the knowledge. Therefore, I searched in Google for "Bitcoin Certification". I was curious to see if there was a formal degree or certification you could receive on Bitcoin and as I suspected there was a program called the Certified Bitcoin Professional. This program sounded exactly like what I was looking for, so I went straight online to Udemy to see if there were any preparation classes for this certification. I bought and downloaded about three classes for about $10 each and went through them all until I could pass the practice tests. I was serious about learning everything I could about this new technology and industry because I knew that Bitcoin and blockchain were going to open so many new doors in the future of so many industries.

This is where I ran across Andreas Antonopoulos. I had heard people speak of him and his book and I had heard him speak on Pomp's podcast and on Perter McCormack's podcast. I heard Andreas mention his Bitcoin Certified Professional preparation course. Turns out that he had a free YouTube video of him teaching a Bitcoin Certified Professional prep class to a live audience. I found the YouTube video and it had a link to a .pdf slide show of his presentation as well.

Andreas' course covered the following and much more:

- History of Bitcoin
- Units of account (satoshis) & Issuance
- Monetary Characteristics
- Transaction basics: inputs, outputs, change
- Keys & Addresses
- Blockchain Explorers
- Price Discovery, Markets and Exchanges
- Transaction Fees & Confirmations
- Basics of Mining
- Consensus

(8)

I appreciated Andreas because he knows the technical side of Bitcoin inside and out, but he found a way to communicate these complex topics within Bitcoin in a way that anyone could understand them. That is not an easy thing to do, but he did it when giving podcast interviews and he did it while teaching his Bitcoin Certified Professional prep course. On the other hand, Andreas' book *Mastering Bitcoin* was perfect for the most advanced technical professionals, but not so great for the average non-technical person. I looked at the reviews of his book and they all basically concurred that this is the best book on the market if you really want to know the nuts and bolts of Bitcoin and the blockchain. If you are serious about understanding the technology, this is the only book you will need. The reviewers say that it was professionally written and quite easy to follow. (54)

Other Bitcoin education books have similar problems. Because Bitcoin is so complex behind the curtains, the subject matter is hard to translate to a lay audience. However, besides my book of course, if you are new to Bitcoin, I suggest you read #**RabbitHoleResource** - *The Bitcoin Standard* by Saifedean Ammous. He does go into the weeds about what money is, but he does it in a non-technical way. One surprising aspect of this book is that a minority of it is spent discussing Bitcoin and blockchain. The majority is spent on the financial history of the world with special focus on the Gold Standard, modern financial catastrophes and their causes, and the relatively recent end of the Gold Standard. I listened to the audio version and I very much enjoyed it.

Saifedean spends a lot of time dwelling on what constitutes sound money and what is unsound money. Essentially, he says that unsound money is money that is not backed by a tangible commodity that will retain its value. Unsound money loses value over time. The US dollar, according to Saifedean, is unsound money as it loses value every year due to planned and unplanned inflation. (55)As we have seen recently, governments can literally print money to pay their debts and he states that the US does this regularly. He further illustrates how banks have the power to create money out of thin air every time they make a new loan, as long as they respect the leverage ratio mandated by banking regulators. This is called fractional reserve banking. This creation of money by bank loans can lead to credit bubbles like the one we saw in 2008.

Saifedean did a great job explaining the Bitcoin network and how bitcoin could function as a reserve currency. He also foresees the emergence of bitcoin banks that hold custody of your bitcoin and settle transactions between banks. He does not expect the average user to be responsible for the custody of their bitcoin.

Saifedean also discussed blockchain in the large altcoins. He does not believe that blockchains can be used to represent real world assets such as real estate or stock equity. This is where I disagree with him. I strongly believe that we will in time tokenize most real-world assets on blockchains, but it will take a lot of technical and legal infrastructure to get us there. For example, I believe eventually all stocks and bonds will be tokenized on the blockchain along with most real estate transactions.

A person cannot complete their initial Bitcoin research without reading the Bitcoin whitepaper and understand who Satoshi Nakamoto is and who Satoshi Nakamoto is not. This was the last pieces of my initial education puzzle.

I had been avoiding looking at the whitepaper because I feared it was going to be too technical. Well I was right, although professionally I come from a technical background, the Bitcoin whitepaper was still too technical for me. I was surprised however that it was less than ten pages. I read it and got the general idea of the paper, but I know others could really appreciate the concepts better and see the genius of this new technology.

In the crypto community there is a lingering mystery as to who is Satoshi Nakamoto. After listening to hours of podcast interviews and discussion treads on Reddit, I've pieced together that Satoshi Nakamoto is nothing more than a pseudonym that was used by the Bitcoin's creator in email communications, forum posts and publications such as the Bitcoin whitepaper. For all we know, this could have been a male, a female, or a group of persons. The name is clearly of Japanese origin, but since the person was writing in perfect English, many believe that Satoshi comes from an English-speaking country.

On the other hand, some Bitcoin O.G. Cypherpunks say that email records indicate that Satoshi was a single person. The Cypherpunks who kept in touch with Nakamoto would describe him as a paranoid fellow. He would be nowhere to be found for days, and then he would start sending out dozens of emails on Fridays. They said that Satoshi was worried that somebody might break Bitcoin, or something might go wrong with it. All in all, this gives a feeling that Satoshi Nakamoto was a coder.

There have been many theories relating Satoshi Nakamoto with programming personalities, such as Hal Finney (rest in peace) and Nick Szabo. However, they both deny any connection to Satoshi. On the other hand, Craig Steven Wright has been actively claiming that he is the real Satoshi Nakamoto. In 2019, he was involved in an active lawsuit surrounding this claim. However, he has failed to present any tangible proof that he is the real Satoshi.

It is commonly believed that we might never find out who Satoshi Nakamoto is and most Bitcoiners want to keep it that way. However, it is clear that this person inadvertently changed the course of history, bringing forward the first digital currency based on blockchain technology. Because of Satoshi's innovation, he launched a new generation of cryptocurrency enthusiast.

CHAPTER 5

Key #2 – Build and Work in Bitcoin

The 7 Superpowers of Bitcoin:

#5 – IMMUTABLE

Immutable refers to the power of Bitcoin that makes it resistant to change. It creates the ability for the Bitcoin blockchain ledger to remain a permanent, indelible, and unalterable history of transactions. Immutable transactions make it impossible for any entity such as a government or corporation, to manipulate, replace, or falsify data stored on the network. Since all historical transactions can be audited at any point in time, immutability enables a high degree of data integrity, both in its technical and primary definition. With Bitcoin immutability, we can prove that the information we present, and use, has not been tampered with.

Today is November 30, 2019. The price for a full bitcoin is $7,569.63 and bitcoin's market cap is $136.8B. We are still early. Bitcoin still not dead.

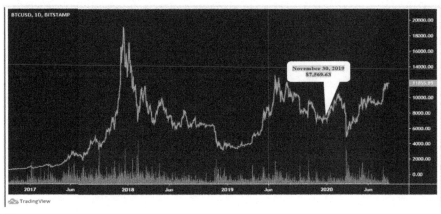

(1)

Here in Cleveland, Ohio, on Lake Erie, it is beginning to get cold and grey as we slowly march towards Winter. That can also describe my crypto mood. I am twenty-one months into my crypto journey, and it has been a roller coaster ride so far. I seem to get seasonal depression and it feels like we are still in the extended crypto winter of 2018. Just a few months ago in the Summer, the bitcoin price peaked at $14K, but every day since, it has slowly grinded down fifty percent to the $7K range of today. Yes, this is better than the $3K range of last year but come on. The chart experts say that we should bounce up off this fifty percent price retracement. But you know what, right now, price is still no longer a daily concern for me. In fact, I really consider the price action as noise. Once you look past the noise you will discover the signal. Last year at this time is when I noticed all the investment and building in the crypto space that the big institutions were supporting. That momentum has not stopped. Therefore, I still have confidence that the orange coin number will go back up.

November 30th is another family birthday. This time it is my only sister's birthday. I never know what gift to give anyone. Traditionally I will get her a birthday card and a gift card to her favorite store for her birthday but this year I have a new idea. You guessed it, I created a bitcoin wallet address and sent $100 USD worth of bitcoin (BTC) to it. Who does not like money, especially the best form of money? I still got her the birthday card and gift card too, but this gift of bitcoin will prove the most valuable when I give it to her. But that is just it. I am saving it for now. I will surprise her later.

Although I have been on my crypto journey for twenty-one months, I still have not really shared my journey with my family and friends except for with my wife and one of my sons and that is only because my son found crypto on his own journey around the same time as I. Last week was Thanksgiving and I still do not find Bitcoin as table conversation yet. I remember stories of how everyone was discussing Bitcoin on Thanksgiving of 2017 right before the Bull Run of 2017. However, not this time for me. I have my conviction, but I am still not ready to be responsible for advising others on Bitcoin and crypto. The last thing I want is for someone to follow me off a cliff. Every time I think about sharing my journey publicly with my friends and family, the price of bitcoin continues to go down and for a new person, that is all they are going to see and probably get discouraged and turn against it forever. They are not going to know of the seven superpowers of bitcoin. Therefore, right now, I continue my journey alone.

2019 has been one of those years. Next week is the second annual Blockland Solutions crypto conference in Cleveland, Ohio, but I do not have a ticket this year. The conference is being held in the Huntington Convention Center, right next door to my job. I hear it is another year of impressive guest speakers. My bank is in cost saving mode, so attending unnecessary conferences are out of the question. I am only glad to see that Cleveland is still pressing forward with their aim to be a premier hub for blockchain companies. Who knows, one day Cleveland, Ohio may become the Silicon Valley of the Mid West.

Speaking of Silicon Valley, my Director who got me the tickets for the Blockland Solutions conference in 2018, decided to leave the bank this Summer and he took another Director's job with another bank in San Francisco. He was falling down the Bitcoin rabbit hole too. He was glad to be out West around all the innovators in the Bitcoin and crypto space. He told me that he was scheduling meetings with companies to bring an idea to life that he had surrounding blockchain and the banking industry. He certainly went to the right place for forward thinking. If you look at most of the crypto startups in the US, most seem to come out of Silicon Valley. That seems so appropriate. Crypto is a disruptive technology designed to be an alternative to the fiat monetary system and fundamentally challenge countless industries. I feel that over the next twenty years, the crypto space will compete with incumbent financial services and banking institutions and crypto businesses are poised to capture the customer growth.

Before my Director left for California, I was basically a unicorn at my bank. You see, I was a Black male Manager, I reported directly to another Black male Director, who reported directly to another Black male Executive Manager. I was the only person in the company that could say that (probably ever). Once my former Director left for Silicon Valley, he was replaced by a White female, so my unicorn status was broken. I had it for about a year and a half. It is exceedingly rare to find Black men in high leadership positions in traditional banking, especially a succession of them.

This is why I say that building and working in the twenty-first century crypto ecosystem is the second key to solving the problems that I laid out in the crypto space. Learning and education is the first key and, building and working in Bitcoin is the second. Participation in the creation of the infrastructure and foundations of the crypto ecosystem is another way that underrepresented women and minorities can gain exposure to the Bitcoin and crypto space. Start your own crypto company or build your own Bitcoin application. If you are not an engineer or technology professional, just take a marketing job, sales position, or administrative assistance position within these new crypto companies. These new companies will have demand for all positions, and it will give you exposure to the industry and give you a competitive advantage. This is a brand-new world that is awakening. Racial diversity and financial inclusion are a good thing for cryptocurrency and blockchain. However, the industry has a lot of work to do and we can help it. Women and minority STEM students have a great opportunity now to enter the crypto space.

I believe that crypto has the potential to allow Black people and all underrepresented citizens to opt out of what some described as a racist financial system on Wall Street. I believe we, as Black people, need to make sure we use censorship-resistant and scarce-money systems such as Bitcoin. Additionally, Black people and all underrepresented people must be part of the development of this new technology. For generations, Black voices and influencers have been suppressed and overlooked in just about every business industry. Black people and Black communities have constantly had to fight for an end to racial, social, and economic oppression. There is a crypto meme that says, "Bitcoin Fixes This".

My fellow Black Bitcoiner and **#BlackExcellence** – author Isaiah Jackson, founder of KRBE Digital Assets Group and author of "Bitcoin & Black America" said that he believes that,

> *"Black investment in digital assets would create a more resilient system than Black Wall Street."* (56)

Black Wall Street was a Black business district that was burned down by white mobs during the Tulsa race massacre of 1921. Isaiah went on further to say,

> *"You can't burn down cryptocurrency and blockchain technology."*

I purchased and read Isaiah's book, *Bitcoin & Black America* as soon as it came out in July of 2019. I love that he dedicated his book to **#BlackExcellence** – Ermias "Nipsey Hussle" Asghedom, may he rest in peace. Nipsey was another young influential Black voice in the Black community who understood the importance of Bitcoin. Isaiah's book was another influence that encouraged me to tell my story and encourage others in the Black and Brown community to adopt bitcoin. I felt that if more diverse voices were heard coming out of the Bitcoin community, the more the minority community would trust and believe the message.

In the crypto world, there are many metaphors and analogies. The building of the internet is often touted as the closest analogy to the building of the Bitcoin and crypto ecosystem. The internet was a fundamentally disruptive and paradigm shifting technology, which forever changed the way the public interacted, communicated, and conducted commerce with each other. So far, crypto is exhibiting the analogous societal change, and thus I expect its growth trend to mimic that of the internet.

I remember when I joined my bank in 1995, not many people had email addresses or an internet connected computer, unless it was at work. However, five years later in 2000, just about everyone I know had the internet at home and a personal email address. My first personal email address was scum5@compuserve.com, a young internet company that has gone by the way. Once the main infrastructure in the crypto ecosystem is built, I expect the same type of exponential growth. We are just waiting to see what that killer app or infrastructure will be that will spur the mass adoption. You may be the one to build it.

Currently, reports vary about user adoption of crypto in the US However, in the surveys that I have seen, the crypto adoption numbers have always been between approximately two percent and five percent. Although Bitcoin is eleven years old and has come a long way, it has yet to see that exponential growth in terms of user adoption. Bitcoin developers are currently working through issues of scalability, privacy, and ease of use, which are all things the internet had to overcome as well, before it reached its full maturity. If you are old enough to remember, the cell phone had similar issues when it hit the market, but today practically everyone around the world has a cell phone. Wonder if you were one of the first employees to work at the first cell phone company. How would your life be different now if you would have made the right decisions and knew the cell phone would be a tool used by everyone in the world. Assuming Bitcoin's growth story follows that of the internet and the cell phone, Bitcoin is positioned to achieve user adoption between twenty percent and fifty percent by the year 2030, right there in the middle of my 2020 – 2040 time frame when I say that the mass adoption of Bitcoin and other digital assets will create a new class of wealth for the current and incoming generations of new financial investors and entrepreneurs. As a result, we must make sure that diverse voices are represented, unlike what happened with the internet and cell phone twenty years ago when it was really created by one demographic and benefitted by one demographic.

I encourage minority voices such as **#BlackExcellence** – Pariss Athena (as known on Twitter) to join the Bitcoin and digital asset movement. Pariss Athena is the creator of the Twitter hashtag **#BlackTechTwitter** and she is the founder of Black Tech Pipeline. With her platform that helps to elevate the profile of Black people working in the tech industry, and to draw more Blacks into it, she can really be a catalyst for Black technology professionals getting into the Bitcoin, crypto, and blockchain space as technology professionals.

The building of the Bitcoin and crypto ecosystem is also analogized with the Gold Rush of the 1840s and the building of the West. When building the wild West, the companies that gained the most were not the ones who were mining for gold, instead they were the ones who sold the actual and proverbial picks and shovels. A current pick-and-shovel company is a company that sells products needed for a larger, overarching industry to operate.

Subsequently, many multi-billion-dollar companies have been built by providing tools as "pick and shovel" opportunities, a reference to Mark Twain's famous line,

> *"When everyone is looking for gold, it's a good time to be in the pick and shovel business."* (57)

The metaphor dates to the mid-19th century. At the time, a man by the name of James W. Marshall had famously discovered gold at Sutter's Mill in California. Word of his discovery spread quickly, drawing in some 300,000 prospectors to the West Coast and sparking what we now know as the California Gold Rush.

You would have thought that it was the gold miners who were the wealthiest people out West but instead it was the companies that supplied the gold miners with picks and shovels and jeans! Levi

Strauss was a big winner of that time. The Levi's story is the stuff of legend. During the California gold rush of the late 1870s, Jacob Davis and Levi Strauss wanted to cash-in on the action, but they did not grab their tin pans and head for the hills. The two men invented the work pants we know today as jeans.

Levi's sold picks and shovels and pants, of course. Those who set up shop early selling mining tools saw a steady stream of income without having to roll the dice on any single mine. Hence the birth of the investing term "picks and shovels." This important business metaphor can help our current builders in the crypto space to navigate the waters of their business model. The Pick and shovel business model is less glamorous sometimes, but the consistent upside has a larger chance of success. There is no difference today. We are at the early stages of building the new digital asset economy. Many of the pioneers have started laying the foundation but there is so much work to be done.

For the twenty-first century gold 2.0 rush, technology engineers are needed. Company founders are racing to become that next Amazon or Google. Crypto jobs are opening, and the demand is filling them quickly. New skill sets are needed. This is a great opportunity for the new generations of tech-savvy young professionals who are ages 16-36 and may aspire to be entrepreneurs, academics, and thoughts leaders in the burgeoning digital business and fintech space. It is time to follow the lead of the early entrepreneurs and the big institutional Wall Street investors.

The big guys got into the game early and now they have a head start. However, this does not have to continue to be a problem. This is only a problem now because the average guy is being left behind. Now is the time to level the playing field. It is time for women and minority STEM students to aggressively adopt blockchain development. We need representation in the infrastructure building, the application building, and the code and smart contract development.

On November 30, the end of 2019, we see that the building of the digital asset economy has been quietly underway for a while. Give yourself one point for each company below that you have heard about before reading it today. These are one hundred US pick and shovel companies in this new digital asset economy. Thousands more companies are waiting to be built or waiting for engineers to make them go. These are also one hundred US companies that have a marketing department, a sales department, human resources, communications, investor relations, technology support, and everything else you will find in a traditional company. The only difference is that these companies have chosen to position themselves toward the future and build their business around a technology that was built for the twenty-first century internet. Therefore, whether you build your own crypto company or app or just work for one of these companies, you can gain valuable knowledge and exposure to this young growing industry at the ground floor level. To most people, this is a once in a lifetime opportunity.

As described in TechCrunch Crunchbase: (58):

#	Company	Founded	Description
1	Abra	2014	Abra is a digital wallet which supports bitcoin and over 50 fiat currencies.
2	Airswap	2017	AirSwap is a decentralized trading network powered by Ethereum.
3	Algorand	2017	Algorand is a scalable, secure and decentralized digital currency and transactions platform.
4	Augur	2014	Augur is an open-source, decentralized prediction market platform.
5	Ausum Ventures	2018	Ausum Blockchain Fund is a hybrid venture and hedge fund comprised of early-stage startups and crypto-assets for social good.
6	Bakkt	2018	Bakkt is a financial services company that focuses on digital currency that specializes in concurrency, rewards, and loyalty points.

7	Bitbounce	2014	BitBounce is a cryptocurrency spam solution that charges unsolicited email senders a Credo fee to send the user their emails.
8	Bitgo	2013	BitGo is the leader in institutional digital asset financial services, providing clients with security, custody, and liquidity solutions.
9	Bitpay	2011	BitPay provides enterprise-grade bitcoin payment solutions for businesses and organizations.
10	Bittrex Support	2014	Bittrex Support operates as a digital asset trading platform.
11	Bitwage	2014	Jobs and Wages for Remote Workers and Dev Shops
12	Blockarray	2016	Block Array is focused on developing blockchain based solutions for the Trucking and Logistics industries.
13	Blockfolio	2014	Blockfolio offers mobile portfolio tracking and management for the cryptocurrency and blockchain industry.
14	Blockstack	2013	Blockstack is a decentralized computing network where users are in control of their data and logins.
15	Blocktower Capital	2017	A leading cryptocurrency investment firm, bringing professional trading and portfolio management to an emerging digital asset class.
16	Blockware Solutions	2017	Blockware Solutions is a blockchain infrastructure company that provides bitcoin and cryptocurrency mining services.

17	Blockworks group	2018	An events and media company on a mission to help investors and executives understand blockchain and digital assets.
18	Bloqboard	2018	Bloqboard is a digital asset lending platform for loans originated and settled on the Ethereum blockchain.
19	Bloxroute Labs	2017	BloXroute is a blockchain distribution network to help your blockchains scale to thousands of transactions/second on-chain.
20	Brave	2015	Brave Software focuses on increasing browsing speed and safety for users, while growing ad revenue share for content creators.
21	BTCS	2013	BTCS (OTCQB: BTCS) is an early mover in the blockchain and digital currency ecosystems
22	Casa	2016	Casa is a startup that helps consumers securely store cryptocurrencies.
23	Chain	2014	Chain builds cryptographic ledger systems that make financial services smarter, more secure, and more connected
24	Chainalysis	2014	Chainalysis helps government agencies, cryptocurrency businesses, and financial institutions engage confidently with cryptocurrency.
25	Chainlink	2019	Chainlink provides reliable tamper-proof inputs and outputs for complex smart contracts on any blockchain.
26	Cindicator	2015	Hybrid Intelligence for effective asset management

27	Circle	2013	Circle is a global internet finance company, built on blockchain technology and powered by crypto assets.
28	Citdex	2016	Citdex is a global multi-strategy applied venture Investment firm inexorably focused on innovative technologies and funds.
29	Civic	2015	Civic's blockchain based ecosystem gives businesses and individuals the tools to control and protect identities.
30	Coin Desk	2013	CoinDesk provides news and analysis on the trends, changes, technologies, companies, and people in the Bitcoin and digital currency world.
31	Coinalytics Co.	2013	Coinalytics is a venture-backed startup that provides real-time intelligence for decentralized blockchain platforms.
32	Coinbase	2012	Coinbase is a digital currency wallet service that allows traders to buy and sell bitcoin.
33	CoinCap	2015	CoinCap.io is a realtime crypto-currency market data, and is now available for iOS devices.
34	Coinflip	2015	CoinFlip is a Bitcoin ATM operator that supports the buying and selling of nine different cryptocur-rencies.
35	Coinlist	2017	CoinList provides a platform for digital asset companies to run their token sales.
36	Coinmine	2018	Coinmine One is the first all-in-one crypto miner for everyone.

37	Coinshares	2017	CoinShares is a digital asset management firm that provides financial products and services for professional investors.
38	Cointele-graph	2013	Cointelegraph covers fintech, blockchain, and Bitcoin, bringing the latest news and analyses on the future of money.
39	Compound	2017	Compound is an open-source interest rate protocol that unlocks new financial applications.
40	Coventure	2011	CoVenture is a multi-asset manager that invests in venture capital, credit, and crypto.
41	Cryptagon	2017	Bringing clarity to crypto holdings
42	Crypto Briefing	2017	Crypto Briefing exists to advocate for the safe and responsible integration of blockchain and cryptocurrency into mainstream life.
43	Crypto Insiders	2018	Crypto Insiders is an online platform that provides a controlled outlet to the jumble of Reddit pages, Telegram chats, and tech blogs.
44	Crypto.IQ	2017	Come join us for the ultimate insider's guide to investing in cryptocurrencies with confidence, by Charlie Shrem and Randall Oser.
45	Delphi Digital	2018	Delphi Digital is an independent research boutique providing institutional-grade analysis on the digital asset market.
46	Digital Asset Holdings	2014	Digital Asset develops distributed ledger technology intended to build distributed, encrypted straight through processing tools.

47	Digital Currency Group	2011	At Digital Currency Group, we build and support bitcoin and blockchain companies by leveraging our insights, network, and access to capital.
48	Distributed Global	2017	Distributed Global is an asset management company exclusively focused on digital and blockchain-based assets.
49	Dsdaq	2019	Dsdaq is a pioneer global trading platform backed by world-class investors, board members and advisors.
50	dydx	2017	dYdX is a decentralized platform offering collateralized lending, borrowing and margin trading for your Ethereum-based assets
51	Filecoin	2014	Filecoin is a data storage network and electronic currency based on Bitcoin.
52	Galaxy Digital	2018	Galaxy Digital as a full service, digital assets merchant bank, with distinct trading, asset management, and principal investment.
53	Gemini	2014	Gemini is a licensed digital asset exchange and custodian built for both individuals and institutions.
54	Greyscale	2013	Grayscale Investments is a leader in digital currency investing
55	Harbor	2017	Harbor is helping to power the next big wave in capital markets – tokenized securities - by automating regulatory compliance.

56	Hyperledg-er	2015	Hyperledger is an open source collaborative effort created to advance cross-industry blockchain technologies.
57	Kadena	2016	Kadena provides a hybrid blockchain platform, including the only scalable layer-1 PoW public network.
58	Kraken	2011	Kraken is a cryptocurrency exchange that provides spot and futures trading between Bitcoin, Ethereum and 30+ other digital assets.
59	Lightning Labs	2016	Lightning Labs is building the next generation of decentralized, resilient financial infrastructure.
60	Lolli	2018	Lolli is a rewards application that allows users to earn bitcoin when shopping online.
61	Lukka	2014	Lukka is a next-generation software company that delivers the leading middle and back office solution for the crypto asset ecosystem.
62	Messari	2018	Messari's mission is to promote transparency and smarter decision-making in the cryptoasset community.
63	Monarch Token	2018	Monarch is the ultimate crypto payment solution for both business and consumers.
64	Nebula Genomics	2016	Nebula Genomics leverages blockchain technology to eliminate middlemen and empower people to own their personal genomic data.

65	Nomics	2017	Nomics is the internet's home page for Bitcoin, Ethereum, and other cryptocurrencies.
66	Nucyher	2015	NuCypher is a cryptography company that builds privacy-preserving infrastructure and protocols.
67	Numerai	2015	Numerai transforms and regularizes financial data into machine learning problems for global network of data scientists.
68	Okcoin	2013	OKCoin provides fiat trading with major digital assets, including Bitcoin, Bitcoin Cash, Ethereum, Ethereum Classic, and Litecoin.
69	Open Finance network	2014	OpenFinance Network is the leading trading platform for tokenized securities.
70	Opensea	2017	OpenSea is a peer-to-peer marketplace for crypto goods.
71	OpSkins	2015	OPSkins Marketplace is an online trading platform, where gamers around the world buy and sell digital items using real-life money.
72	Opyn	2019	Opyn is building an insurance marketplace to protect cryptocurrency users against system risks in Decentralized Finance.
73	Orchid Labs	2017	Orchid Labs is an open-source project committed to ending surveillance and censorship on the internet.
74	Paxos	2012	Paxos is a regulated financial institution building infrastructure to enable movement between physical and digital assets.

75	Pei	2017	Unlock automatic cashback in Bitcoin or USD on your debit or credit cards!
76	Picks and Shovels	2017	The Picks & Shovels Co. crafting tools for investors and traders of digital currencies and crypto assets.
77	Poloniex	2014	Poloniex is a cryptocurrency exchange with advanced trading features.
78	R3	2014	R3 is a financial innovation firm dedicated to the design and deployment of DLT to build the new operating system for financial services.
79	Ripple	2012	Ripple provides one frictionless experience to send money globally using the power of blockchain.
80	Satoshi Capital Advisors	2018	Satoshi Capital is an algorithmic trading company, specializing in alpha generation and providing liquidity to cryptocurrency exchanges.
81	Satoshi Nakamoto Institute	2014	Satoshi Nakamoto mined the first block of the Bitcoin blockchain, kickstarting the world's first fully realized crypto-currency.
82	Securrency	2015	Securrency delivers financial technology products for the tokenized issuance and trading of securities..
83	Seed Cx	2015	Seed CX provides institutional investors and professional traders with the market structure and technology.

84	Shapeshift	2014	ShapeShift is a crypto platform, enabling customers to buy, sell, trade, track, send, receive, and interact with their digital assets.
85	Sharespost	2009	SharesPost is a company that provides liquidity solutions in the private growth asset market.
86	Spring Labs	2017	Spring Labs is a transformative and decentralized infrastructure for credit and identity data.
87	Swarm Fund	2014	Swarm Fund is the blockchain for private equity, opening up access to the new digital economy.
88	Tagomi	2018	Tagomi is the First Electronic Prime Broker in Crypto. Trading, Custody, Margin, Lending, Shorting, Staking, Financing, all in one account.
89	TaxBit	2018	TaxBit is a cryptocurrency tax calculation and withholding service that serves investors, exchanges, and payment services.
90	Tendermint	2014	Tendermint brings simplicity, security, and speed to the world's blockchains.
91	Tidbit	2015	The one-way notification app.
92	Tokensoft	2017	TokenSoft is a technology and security platform that automates the asset management and fundraising experience.
93	Uphold	2014	Uphold enables 1.5MM+ members worldwide to buy, sell and send various forms of value through one simple interface.

94	Vault12	2014	Vault12 is the first to deliver decentralized digital custody to protect your most precious digital assets.
95	Vertalo	2017	Vertalo is a SaaS solution connecting and enabling the digital asset economy.
96	Vosai	2018	VOSAI is a decentralized machine learning infrastructure focused on computer vision and natural languages.
97	Voyager	2017	Voyager is a crypto asset broker that provides retail and institutional investors with a turnkey solution.
98	Wachsman	2015	Wachsman provides first class professional services to fintech innovators, rising entrepreneurs and blockchain businesses.
99	Wibson	2017	Wibson is a decentralized data marketplace empowering individuals to monetize their data, safely.
100	Wyre	2013	Wyre is replacing banking technologies that have been stagnant for 30+ years.

CHAPTER 6

Key # 3 – Acquire Bitcoin

The 7 Superpowers of Bitcoin:

#6 – TRANSPARENT

Transparent is bitcoin's power to offer unprecedented transaction search capabilities. Bitcoin works with an unprecedented level of transparency that most people are not used to dealing with. All bitcoin transactions are public, traceable, and permanently stored in the Bitcoin network. Bitcoin addresses are the only information used to define where bitcoin is allocated and where they are sent. These addresses are created privately by each user's wallets. Anyone can see the balance and all transactions of any address. Anyone can search for information based on bitcoin addresses, block numbers and transaction hashes.

Happy Birthday Bitcoin! Today is January 3, 2020. The price for a full bitcoin is $7,344.88 and bitcoin's market cap is $133.2B. We are still early. Bitcoin still not dead.

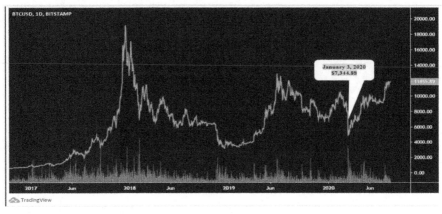

(1)

It is January 3, 2020 and I am twenty-two months into my crypto journey. I know, I know, we just checked in a month ago on November 30, 2019 when it was my sister's birthday. Well, I could not let this check in go by because now it is Bitcoin's birthday and she is eleven years old. As I put that into perspective, I just had my eleven-year Twitter anniversary. Running through my mind is, how in the world did I know about Twitter in 2009 but did not know about Bitcoin? This demonstrates that even in the early days, Jack Dorsey proved to be a very crafty CEO to be able to get me interested in a new social platform at the same time a revolutionary financial technology was being introduced to the world by Satoshi Nakamoto. Regardless, it is amazing how eleven years later, Bitcoin, Twitter, and Square (Cash App), would be linked in so many ways.

However, before I go any farther in this chapter, I must remind you that I am not an Investment Advisor. This chapter is for informational, educational, and entertainment purposes only. No information contained in this chapter constitutes tax, legal, insurance or investment advice.

This chapter should not be considered a solicitation, offer or recommendation for the purchase or sale of any cryptocurrency, security, or any other financial products and services discussed herein.

Readers of this chapter should know that bitcoin is very volatile. You should do your own research before deciding to invest your money and know that you can lose all your money.

Readers of this chapter should not construe any discussion or information contained herein as personalized advice from me or the publisher. Readers should discuss the personal applicability of the specific products, services, strategies, or issues posted herein with a professional advisor of his or her choosing.

Information throughout this chapter, whether asset quotes, charts, articles, or any other statement or statements regarding capital markets or other financial information, is obtained from sources which I, believe reliable, but I do not warrant or guarantee the timeliness or accuracy of this information. Neither our information providers nor I shall be liable for any errors or inaccuracies, regardless of cause, or the lack of timeliness of, or for any delay or interruption in, the transmission thereof to the user. With respect to information regarding financial performance, nothing in this chapter should be interpreted as a statement or implication that past results are an indication of future performance.

Now that I have pleased my lawyers and got that out of the way, I can discuss the theme of this chapter: Stacking Sats (Satoshis)! In chapters four and five I talked about how participating in the mass adoption of Bitcoin through learning and building, would create solutions to the problematic issues we discussed in chapters one – three. In this chapter I present a third solution to the problems: Acquiring and Owning Bitcoin. For me, this solution was where the real fun came in to play. It was time for me to put skin in the game and acquire some bitcoin.

I acquired my first bitcoin in April of 2018, and as they say, the rest is history. I quickly fell down the rabbit hole. It is hard to describe, but owning bitcoin felt like freedom. It was refreshing. I so regret that I was nine years late to purchasing my first satoshi but, I feel fortunate that in retrospect, I was still early. It was not too late. I was a true early adopter.

Everyone that comes into Bitcoin feels that they are too late. There are people who purchased bitcoin at $8.00 in 2011 who swore that they were late, and the game was over. This is my favorite Tweet from a user in 2011.

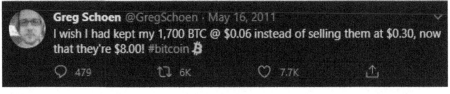

Greg Schoen @GregSchoen · May 16, 2011
I wish I had kept my 1,700 BTC @ $0.06 instead of selling them at $0.30, now that they're $8.00! #bitcoin ₿

  479   6K   7.7K

(59)

I find similar examples of people who purchased at $300, $1,000, and $3,000. In a manner of five years from today, I am going to look back and realize just how early a price of $7,000 really was. Therefore, now is always the best time to consider owning bitcoin. You do not want to let another eleven years go by before you come around to reality. By then, in 2031, the price of one full bitcoin could be well over $500,000 or close to $1,000,000.

My whole thesis of this book centers on the fact that I believe that it is now time for the average consumer to be financially curious and that curiosity should lead you to realize that you do not know enough about what money is and how to make it work for you. You should also know that this is by design. The current money system is solely controlled by the government and they do not want the average citizen to know the ends and outs of how they manipulate the money supply.

However, fortunately for us, Bitcoin is an alternative to the traditional financial system. It is a new revolutionary financial technology for the twenty-first century global consumer who wants a better form of money for the future. Bitcoin is intended to be the people's internet money and over the next twenty years, bitcoin will be the vehicle that will level the financial playing field for underrepresented women, minorities, and average joe investors, if and only if, they take advantage of the early adopter advantage that today's current time offers. Today's early advantage will separate the "Haves" from the "Have Nots" of the future.

The question becomes, how do you convince a "Nocoiner" to leave the status quo and comfort of the traditional financial system? That answer can be somewhat complicated. There are two lines of thought in the Bitcoin community: HODL or Spend. Both lines of thought are on the same page as to stacking satoshis. They both believe that you should acquire as many satoshis or bitcoin that your investment tolerance can take. For some conservative investors that may be only one percent to five percent of their disposable income. This is your income after you pay all your debts and monthly expenses. We are still early. The bitcoin and crypto markets are still volatile, so most prudent advisors advise that you only invest as much as you can comfortably afford to lose. If someone loses one percent to five percent of their disposable income, that will probably not ruin that person financially forever. On the other hand, due to the asymmetrical nature of the crypto market, a one percent allocation could turn into a 1,000% to 10,000% gain. So, a small allocation is generally worth the risk. For those individuals who have extensive crypto literacy and have a higher risk tolerance, I have heard that some people are comfortable with having up to fifty percent or more of their wealth in crypto. I would never recommend that for someone starting new into bitcoin, but my recommendation is always, **DO YOUR OWN RESEARCH**. The bottom line is that everyone in the crypto community believes that a zero percent allocation is not an option. Now is the time to get off zero.

Now where there is disagreement in the Bitcoin community, stems from the decision you make after you acquire your bitcoin. Some people like me feel that currently bitcoin should function as digital gold and just serve as a store of value. We are the HODLers and recommend that one hold their bitcoin and not spend it as you acquire it. As the circulating supply decreases and the demand for bitcoin increases, the law of supply and demand suggests that the price will rise accordingly. We believe that until bitcoin reaches a sufficiently high market cap to which price fluctuations become less volatile, you should HODL. When bitcoin does reach and surpass that sufficient market cap, we believe that bitcoin will then be in a new phase and then can serve as a medium of exchange and unit of account. Only then do we recommend spending your satoshis regularly. I do not know when that day will happen, but when it does, you will know.

Others in the Bitcoin community take the opposite approach. They believe that it is imperative that the community spend their bitcoin now as a currency on retail transactions. They believe that to gain mass adoption, merchants must feel comfortable accepting bitcoin and consumers have to feel comfortable spending bitcoin. They believe that the daily transaction volume in bitcoin should be more than just investment trading activity on crypto exchanges.

Although I am a HODLer, I do agree that we do need some retail transactions in bitcoin as well. Therefore, I would say that I believe in 80/20 HODL to Spend bitcoin. You just never want to look back and be the Bitcoin Pizza Guy. You remember Laslo Hanzecz. In 2010, when bitcoin was priced less than a penny at $0.0025, Laslo wanted to establish that bitcoin could be used for commercial retail purchases, so he spent 10,000 bitcoin, whose current value at the time was $25 US dollars, that he had mined to purchase two pizzas. At the time, that felt like a fair trade because the price of bitcoin was next to nothing. However, the value of 10,000 bitcoin today is $90,000,000 US dollars, making that the most expensive pizza purchase in history and that was only ten years ago. I am sure that Laslo still had much more bitcoin left after his purchase, but I bet an extra $90,000,000 today would make him feel a lot better.

This just demonstrates that when an asset is expected to massively appreciate over time, it is best to hold it till the future. My sincere belief is that bitcoin will reach $100,000 by 2022, $500,000 by 2028, and over $1,000,000 by 2040. Therefore, for me, I will only be spending my bitcoin sparingly unless absolutely necessary. More than likely, I will be using my bitcoin as collateral for other new twenty-first century financial transactions but that is a discussion for another book.

Conversely, when an asset depreciates over time you are incentivized to sell it or spend it. That is the reason the government sets a two percent inflation rate for the US dollar. Because you know that cash does not hold its value, and in fact it loses two percent of its value each year to inflation, this fact is supposed to encourage you to spend your cash to stimulate the economy. This is the reason that rich people do not keep a lot of money in cash, instead they put their money in other assets that appreciate rather than depreciate. Bitcoin also fixes this.

Even publicly traded companies are starting to realize the value of Bitcoin. According to a Forbes article, MicroStrategy has decided to use Bitcoin as the reserve asset on their balance sheet. MicroStrategy is not in the Bitcoin business. They have no blockchain-based products. This is a traditional company that realizes that Bitcoin is an appropriate hedge in uncertain economic times.

MicroStrategy has taken $250 million of their balance sheet capital and purchased 21,454 bitcoin. Michael Saylor, CEO of MicroStrategy, said,

> *"Our investment in Bitcoin is part of our new capital allocation strategy, which seeks to maximize long-term value for our shareholders. This investment reflects our belief that Bitcoin, as the world's most widely-adopted cryptocurrency, is a dependable store of value and an attractive investment asset with more long-term appreciation potential than holding cash. Since its inception over a decade ago, Bitcoin has emerged as a significant addition to the global financial system, with characteristics that are useful to both individuals and institutions. MicroStrategy has recognized Bitcoin as a legitimate investment asset that can be superior to cash and accordingly has made Bitcoin the principal holding in its treasury reserve strategy.*

> *MicroStrategy spent months deliberating to determine our capital allocation strategy. Our decision to invest in Bitcoin at this time was driven in part by a confluence of macro factors affecting the economic and business landscape that we believe is creating long-term risks for our corporate treasury program — risks that should be addressed proactively. Those macro factors include, among other things, the economic and public health crisis precipitated by COVID-19, unprecedented government financial stimulus measures including quantitative easing adopted around the world, and global political and economic uncertainty. We believe that, together, these and*

other factors may well have a significant depreciating effect on the long-term real value of fiat currencies and many other conventional asset types, including many of the assets traditionally held as part of corporate treasury operations."

He goes on to say,

"We find the global acceptance, brand recognition, ecosystem vitality, network dominance, architectural resilience, technical utility, and community ethos of Bitcoin to be persuasive evidence of its superiority as an asset class for those seeking a long-term store of value. Bitcoin is digital gold – harder, stronger, faster, and smarter than any money that has preceded it. We expect its value to accrete with advances in technology, expanding adoption, and the network effect that has fueled the rise of so many category killers in the modern era." (60)

As an individual, regardless of whether you align with HOLDL or Spend, the important part is that you participate and begin to acquire and stack satoshis. There are two main ways for you to acquire bitcoin: Earn Bitcoin or Purchase Bitcoin. Within each of these categories there are several subcategories that make it easy for you to get started.

Let us start with the better way to acquire bitcoin, earning it. There are several ways to earn bitcoin including but not limited to getting paid in bitcoin, selling items for bitcoin, getting rewards in bitcoin, and mining bitcoin. I say these ways are the better ways to acquire bitcoin because for the most part these ways involve more privacy, are less expensive, and do not require you to do anything you do not already normally do. In most instances they do not require you to share your personal information such as your driver's license or passport, which are critical components in know your customer (KYC) and anti-money laundering (AML) requirements of the traditional and regulated crypto financial businesses. Additionally, in many of the earning bitcoin ways, there are no fees.

For instance, if you want to get paid in bitcoin, you can use your labor or skills (barber, car washer, babysitter) and request your customer to pay you in bitcoin. All you need to do is provide them with your bitcoin wallet address where you want to receive the funds. Those can be private commercial transactions that do not involve sharing personal information or fees. An exception to this is if you want to have your W2 income from your employer paid to you in bitcoin. Believe it or not, there are payroll providers services that allow your employer to pay you in bitcoin and your employer does not even have to know about it. For instance, with the company Bitwage, they have a five-step process an employee can take to get paid in bitcoin:

1. The Employee sets up an account with Bitwage.
2. Bitwage issues specific banking details for the user.
3. The employee gives these banking details to their employer or client.
4. Payroll sends a USD wire or direct deposit to the employee's Bitwage banking detail.
5. Bitwage then delivers digital assets directly to the wallet or account of the employee's choice the same day or next day.

You can further earn bitcoin by selling things you own. Andreas Antonopoulos said that he once sold his car for bitcoin. Other people have sold their house. If someone has bitcoin and they are willing to part way with it, they will buy anything of value.

Now me personally, I earn bitcoin two different ways. The first way is through rewards. This is like the cash back reward program that credit card companies offer. Instead of receiving points or cash, you receive bitcoin or satoshis. There are two companies and apps that I use that reward me for my everyday shopping activities. The first company is called **#RabbitHoleResource -** Pei. They have a mobile app that you download. After you link your credit or debit card to the app, it tracks all your spending. If you spend dollars at one of their participating retailers, they give you satoshis back rewards. For example, whenever I purchase anything from the following retailers, I get paid back in bitcoin:

CVS	Macy's	Domino's Pizza
McDonalds	Chick-fil-A	Trader Joe's

Walgreen	Chipotle	Target
Taco Bell	Uber	Dunkin Donuts

And the list of merchants goes on. This is really a clever marketing strategy for Pei and the retailers because it has changed my shopping behavior. When I need to pick up an item from the store, I consciously choose a retailer that I know will reward me in bitcoin. This often decides my lunch time meal.

The company **#RabbitHoleResource** - Lolli is another bitcoin rewards company that I use. Lolli works similar to Pei but instead of brick and mortar shopping, they focus on online shopping retailers. They include over 800 online retailers, everyone from Walmart to Priceline. Each retailer determines the percent of satoshis back that you receive but being rewarded with free money is always a good thing no matter the amount.

With both of my bitcoin reward companies, they allow you to transfer the bitcoin you earn off their platform wallet and into your own personal bitcoin wallet. This allows you to truly own and have responsibility for your own bitcoin. You will not make a living on earning bitcoin rewards, but it does not require you to do anything different than you are already doing. Over a year's time, I received a few hundred dollars in bitcoin rewards passively. The best part of receiving the rewards in satoshis is that the $200 - $300 in rewards that you earn this year may appreciate to $2,000 - $3,000 over a short period of time. This does not happen with your regular cash back programs when you are rewarded in US dollars.

The last way that I personally earn bitcoin is through a form of bitcoin mining. I am not going to get into the technical details of bitcoin mining in this book. That is one of the complex technical subjects within the Bitcoin protocol. I will just say that bitcoin mining is analogous to gold mining, but instead, it is all done by a computer program. The miner must expend some energy to mine a scarce asset. If a miner is successful, then he is then rewarded, in this case, with bitcoin.

I perform bitcoin mining with a retail mining product called a

#RabbitHoleResource - Coinmine One. This was the first purchase that I made where I spent my own bitcoin. On September 22,2019, my Coinmine cost me 0.06461418 BTC. It is like an Xbox or PlayStation that you plug into the wall. Like satoshis back rewards, the Coinmine gives you a passive way to earn bitcoin. My Coinmine was built to order, therefore, it took a few weeks before I received it. However, I plugged my Coinmine into the wall on August 24, 2019, connected it to my wi-fi, and in five minutes I was earning bitcoin. That was it. I do not have to do anything else. I can monitor my bitcoin production on my mobile app. With bitcoin mining you are exchanging electricity for bitcoin. That is it. Again, with one retail bitcoin miner, you are not going to get rich, but you are participating in the bitcoin ecosystem and adding to the security and decentralization nature of the network. This is just another passive way to stack satoshis without changing any of your regular behavior.

Many critics say that the retail miners are a waste of money because they have a poor ROI. However, I do not look at it that way. In less than a year, I have stacked over 2M satoshis passively, without doing anything but plugging a box into the wall. Again, to me the name of the game is stacking satoshis. There is a fixed number of bitcoin. Soon the competition for that bitcoin will heat up. Once the demand outweighs the supply, you know what happens to the price. Therefore, if the satoshis you earn today are not profitable that does not mean that these same satoshis will not be profitable next year or the year after. Bitcoin is a long game. Just remember the Bitcoin Pizza Guy.

The other major way of acquiring bitcoin is to directly purchase bitcoin. The major ways to purchase bitcoin are directly person to person, through a bitcoin ATM, or through a cryptocurrency exchange.

There is a website called Local Bitcoins that brings individual buyers and sellers together peer to peer. This site is like Craigs List and comes with similar risks and dangers of Craigs List. I have personally never used this site. However, for people in certain countries, this may be the best way that they have, to purchase bitcoin. Like anything, you just need to take the proper precautions. I know that some police stations offer Craig List zones in their parking lots, where consumers can meet to engage in peer to peer commerce. You can do the same with meeting someone to exchange Fed dollars for bitcoin. A bank is also a good place to meet. I would advise any place with a lot of cameras, just for your safety, if you need to do it this way.

More and more, bitcoin ATMs are popping up across the United States to give people more options to purchase bitcoin and other cryptocurrencies. These are machines where you can put cash in, and they will return you a bitcoin address with the corresponding amount of bitcoin. In some countries, people can use these machines privately without giving any personal identifying information, however in the US most bitcoin ATMs that I have seen require you to set up an account and give the appropriate KYC and AML information. However, some of these bitcoin ATMs allow you to purchase bitcoin and sell bitcoin for cash if you need it. I have never used the bitcoin ATMs because they do charge significant fees in my opinion and I have other lower cost options that I can use. But like anything, if that is your only option, then it is a good way to acquire bitcoin. In Cleveland, Ohio, I am seeing these bitcoin ATMs pop up in gas stations, mostly in underserved areas. I guess that is a good thing for now.

Now the most popular way to purchase bitcoin is through a traditional cryptocurrency exchange. This is how I first got started in crypto. The first exchange I came across was Coinbase. It was easy to set up an account and get started. Because they are a regulated US cryptocurrency exchange, you do have to provide them with full identifying information just as if you were opening a bank account. In crypto, the process is more streamlined. All you do is upload a photo ID from a driver's license or a passport and hold up a sign with the current date and take a selfie. In a couple of minutes or hours, your account is approved.

At a fiat to crypto exchange, you can buy crypto with dollars then trade that crypto for other crypto if you choose. The better choice in my opinion is to just buy bitcoin and HODL. Most crypto enthusiast will tell you, once you purchase any crypto from an exchange, you should immediately move it off the exchange to a personal wallet. This is where crypto can get a little complex for some users. Now you have to understand the different types of wallets, cold wallets, hot wallets, paper wallets, brain wallets, etc. Then you must worry about managing your own security keys. What is a Key? It is my recommendation that you do take the time to learn these aspects of cryptocurrency before you purchase your first asset. These concepts are especially important. Cryptocurrency forces you to learn personal accountability. There is a phrase in crypto that could not be any truer: Not your keys, not your bitcoin. This means that if you are not in possession of your private keys, then you really do not own the bitcoin.

If you have your bitcoin in a wallet on an exchange, like Coinbase, then Coinbase controls the private keys. If they get hacked or decide that they do not want you to access your bitcoin, then you are out of luck. They are in crypto, but they are still a centralized company and can censor you or shut your account down if they want to. In the early days of bitcoin several cryptocurrency exchanges went out of business due to alleged hacks or strait up fraud. Any user that stored their crypto with those exchanges were out of luck and many had no recourse.

In the United States, the risk of the current regulated cryptocurrency exchanges scamming you or getting hacked is extremely low and most exchanges carry some type of insurance. However, it is best to be safe than sorry and not leave any significant amount of crypto on an exchange. Most people only leave crypto on the exchange if they are an active trader, otherwise they move their assets to a personal wallet until they want to trade it or withdraw it.

The best types of wallets are what they call cold wallets, meaning that they are hardware wallets that are not connected to the internet. Most of them look like a USB stick. I have a **#RabbitHoleResource** - Ledger Nano S wallet. This is a great cryptocurrency cold wallet because it supports several different cryptocurrencies you may purchase, and it has a great user experience interface.

Along my crypto journey I also came across the **#RabbitHoleRe-source** - MyEtherWallet. This is a wallet that will hold cryptocur-rencies that are based on the Ethereum blockchain protocol. This wallet is not a hardware wallet, instead it is software you run on your computer through a website. You controlled your own private keys, which is much better than leaving your keys with a third party, but not quite as secure as an offline hardware wallet.

I also had a couple of mobile wallets that were based on your phone. The company **#RabbitHoleResource** - Blockchain has a good mobile wallet where you manage your own keys. The problem with all these options is that you must keep up with all these different wallets, keys, addresses. The process can become overwhelming, especially if you own several different cryptocurrencies. All of this can be confusing, and many people do prefer the ease of leaving their funds with the exchange or another third party, similar to how they use traditional banks. You must weigh the risk and reward for yourself.

When I started buying crypto back in 2018, Coinbase only had less than five cryptocurrency options. Now they have over thirty. They had bitcoin, Ethereum, Litecoin, and a couple more. However, I was seeing the shiny new cryptocurrencies come around like XRP,

Stellar, and Dash, to name a few. I had to find other cryptocurrency exchanges that sold those other assets. Like I mentioned in an earlier chapter, by the end of 2018, I owned about seventeen different cryptocurrencies besides bitcoin. That required me to open an account with several cryptocurrency exchanges because they all offered different cryptos. Of course, they all offered bitcoin, but if you wanted an exotic new crypto, you had to find it. I had to open an account with #**RabbitHoleResource** - Bitrex, Kucoin, and my favorite exchange, Binance.

Binance was a Chinese exchange that launched in 2017 and rose to become the biggest and most popular exchange by volume in just one year. They had a great user experience and they offered almost every cryptocurrency that came to market. The CEO and founder of Binance, #**RabbitHoleResource** - Changpeng Zhao (CZ for short), is a Crypto Twitter favorite. Unfortunately, US regulations began to ban US citizens from using Binance. Luckily, this was about the time I was exiting all of my altcoins anyway. Binance finally did open a regulated Binance.US exchange in 2019 with a slightly limited offering.

Today, I am a bitcoin only purchaser and no longer use the major crypto exchanges to buy bitcoin. I use a bitcoin only app. I use the Cash App now because they make it easy to purchase and move your bitcoin, and bitcoin is the only crypto that they offer. To me Coinbase is still a good crypto exchange for newer people but for me and some other seasoned people in the bitcoin community, we have turned away from Coinbase once they began to promote the use of various altcoins and some shitcoins. Jack Dorsey from the Cash App has gone on record of saying that he is not interested in offering any other cryptocurrency other than bitcoin. It is great to have the support of a visionary CEO for the mass adoption of bitcoin.

After I purchase my bitcoin from Cash App I HODL it in two places. I move a portion to my personal Ledger Nano S wallet, and I move a portion to a third party provided called BlockFi. Although BlockFi manages my private keys for me, they compensate me for taking that risk. This company offers the type of twenty-first century financial products that the world will soon be accustomed to having. They offer bitcoin interest accounts that pay up to five percent monthly interest. They offer other USD stable coin accounts that pay as much as nine percent APY interest. They also offer crypto backed collateral loans. Therefore, when you need US dollar liquidity you do not have to sell your bitcoin, you can just apply for an instant collateral loan against your bitcoin. These types of forward-looking financial products are just what this new digital economy needs.

In summary, I am not an investment advisor, however, I do believe strongly that it is time for those of us who have been historically underrepresented in the traditional financial system to turn to a financial asset that has the opportunity to change our financial destiny. Do your own research, but as for me, I am going to continue to dollar cost average into bitcoin every week and anytime we get a significant pull back in the bitcoin price, I am buying the dip!

CHAPTER 7

Meet the Excellence Academy

The 7 Superpowers of Bitcoin:

#7 – DISINFLATIONARY

Disinflationary describes the power of bitcoin's monetary policy. Bitcoin has a fixed money supply cap of twenty-one million coins. However, unlike traditional monetary policies, bitcoin's supply schedule is neither inflationary nor deflationary in the long run. It is instead disinflationary, which means that the rate of newly minted bitcoin produced, decreases over time until it reaches zero through an event called the Bitcoin halving. When bitcoin was first mined in 2009, it rewarded the miners fifty bitcoin approximately every ten minutes a block was created. Approximately every four years (or more specifically, every 210,000 blocks) that reward is cut in half. In 2012 the miner reward was cut to twenty-five bitcoin every ten minutes. In 2016 the reward was cut to twelve and a half bitcoin every ten minutes and in May of 2020 the miner reward was cut to six and a quarter bitcoin every ten minutes. Approximately every four years or 210,000 blocks, this process will continue until all twenty-one million coins are mined into circulation. After that, no more bitcoin can be created out of thin air.

Happy Birthday to me again! Today is May 10, 2020. The price for a full bitcoin is $8,756.43 and bitcoin's market cap is $160.9B. We are still early. Bitcoin still not dead.

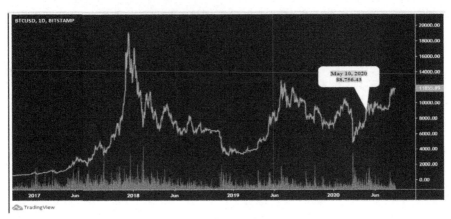

(1)

It has been a wild two-year ride. Some will say this is normal crypto. When we began Chapter one, we looked at bitcoin's price and market cap on May 10, 2018. Today is May 10, 2020. Let us recap the price and market cap movement throughout the chapters.

Chapters:

I) **May 10, 2018**

Bitcoin Price – $9,043.94
Bitcoin Market Cap -- $154.0B

II) **December 16, 2018**

Bitcoin Price – $3,236.76
Bitcoin Market Cap -- $56.7B

III) **July 14, 2019**

Bitcoin Price – $10,256.06
Bitcoin Market Cap -- $182.7B

IV) **October 12, 2019**

Bitcoin Price – $8,336.56
Bitcoin Market Cap -- $150.0B

V) **November 30, 2019**

Bitcoin Price – $7,569.63
Bitcoin Market Cap -- $136.8B

VI) **January 3, 2020**

Bitcoin Price – $7,344.88
Bitcoin Market Cap -- $133.2B

VII)　**May 10, 2020**

Bitcoin Price – $8,756.43
Bitcoin Market Cap -- $160.9B

Day 1 of writing this book, May 13, 2020:

Bitcoin Price – $9,269.99
Bitcoin Market Cap -- $170.4B

I would say that this roller coaster ride will rival any that Cedar Point amusement park has to offer. But just like an amusement park ride, when you get off, you are anxious to get back on. The crypto world provides many such thrills.

Well here we are, May 10, 2020 and like clockwork, the third Bitcoin halving is programmatically scheduled to occur tomorrow on 5/11/2020, and the Bitcoin community is anxiously awaiting and has been counting down for months. We now get to see Bitcoin's Disinflationary superpower in action. This will mark another important milestone in the growth story of Bitcoin. The supply of new bitcoin rewarded to miners every ten minutes will be cut in half to six and a quarter bitcoin per block. This reduction of new supply, coupled with the same or increase in demand for bitcoin, has historically resulted in a massive increase in the price of bitcoin over time. Everyone is expecting no different this time. This programmatic feature of Bitcoin's monetary policy is one aspect that makes bitcoin superior to any other currency in circulation. I was hoping that the Bitcoin halving event fell on my birthday. That would have been the final confirmation I needed to know that Bitcoin and I are meant to be together. Oh well, I missed it by one day. The next Bitcoin halving event will occur 210,000 blocks later, approximately in early 2024 at block height 840,000, when the new reward supply will be cut to 3.125 bitcoin per block.

Anyhow, I am celebrating my birthday today for the third time since I embarked upon my twenty-six-month journey deep into the Bitcoin rabbit hole. Unfortunately, despite the halving event, this birthday is not so festive, since we are still at the early onset of this global pandemic spread of the COVID-19 virus. Fortunately, my wife keeps me and our family in line and ensures that we are safe by isolating ourselves, and when it is necessary to be in public she ensures that we keep social distance of at least six feet from others and wear face coverings. Wow, we are living in a profoundly different world, than just four months ago, that has changed overnight!

With everything going on in the world today resulting from the worldwide COVID-19 pandemic, on this birthday, I am more confident than ever in my knowledge and conviction that Bitcoin is one of the vehicles that the world needs to move steadfast throughout the twenty-first century. This pandemic has taught me and the whole world some quick valuable lessons:

1. We are all globally connected
2. Change can happen slowly, then all at once in an instance
3. Virtual interactions through the internet is going to be the new normal for various life activities
    a. Working from home
    b. Communication through video conference (i.e. Zoom, WebEx)
    c. Move toward contactless Virtual Currency??? YES, Bitcoin solves this

Therefore, this year, my birthday celebration was short-lived because I knew that I had some particularly important work ahead of me that I decided I must begin immediately. Instead of letting this pandemic get me down, I wanted to use this catalyst to motivate me to grow personally and professionally and come out stronger on the other side. I was personally determined to not let our quarantine and isolation depress my spirit.

Every motivational speaker on TV was saying, write a book, or start a business, while you are on quarantine. Okay, so I did both! On May 13, 2020 I started writing my book and by May 17, 2020, I filed my paperwork with the state to incorporate my business and by May 30, 2020, my wife and I signed our Operating Agreement. I could not just keep this to myself. It was now time for me to share my voice, make a difference, and leave a legacy. These last twenty-six months have given me the confidence and taught me that this Bitcoin thing is real, and more people need to know about it and experience all it has to offer. I know that there is no way that all these wealthy and smart people, who I have come across, are wrong about this Bitcoin thesis.

However, I do believe that there is only limited time remaining for the average Main Street citizen to position themselves in front of the mass adoption of Bitcoin to come, but it is not too late if you act now. This is the main message that I want to deliver to the world, and more importantly, to the ones who I care about.

As a result, my wife and I decided to combine her passion for diversity, equity, and inclusion and my passion for Bitcoin and digital finance, and form a startup business with our family that we could utilize to foster our new mission in life.

We would like to introduce you to **#BlackExcellence** – SoFL Excellence Academy, LLC, pronounced South Florida Excellence Academy. This company is our commitment to give back to our community and to leave a legacy for our children and grandchildren. SoFL Excellence Academy is our family-owned business. My wife Angela Johnson is Chief Executive Officer (CEO) and Founding Member. My role is Chief Operating Officer (COO) and Founding Member. My daughter, Asia Saffold is Chief Administrative Officer (CAO). My Sister-in-Law, Dawn Morris is Chief Financial Officer (CFO). We also have a Senior Management team that manages our Talent Acquisition & University Relations, Operations & Project Management, and Instructional Design. We all bring a wealth of talent and passion from our respective careers and backgrounds that fit well with our mission for SoFL Excellence Academy.

The SoFL Excellence Academy is a forward-looking education and training consultancy company. This means that we always have an eye towards the future and the next generations. As such, continuous improvement is an ongoing tenant that underlies our business. Our company utilizes a variety of digital and traditional platforms to educate, train, and encourage the mass adoption of Bitcoin and other forms of digital business and finance. We are a minority and woman-owned business enterprise that we founded in the state of Florida on May 17, 2020. Our main office is headquartered in Pembroke Pines, Florida.

We positioned SoFL Excellence Academy as a premier provider of world-class education, training, and digital content, targeted towards women and minorities in the United States, who have been historically underrepresented in the professional career fields of business, finance, and technology. We further target any individuals in America ages 16 – 36 who may aspire to be entrepreneurs, academics, and thought leaders in the digital asset space. Therefore, we concentrate on attracting young minority and women STEM students, aspiring technology entrepreneurs, rising investment professionals, and Diversity, Equity & Inclusion professionals throughout the United States.

We aim to give our target audience choice, access, empowerment, and freedom to build their financial futures. Our vision is to become the premier, go-to, digital business and fintech preparation company and best incubator of young minority and women entrepreneurs, academics, and thought leaders in the digital business and fintech space.

At SoFL Excellence Academy, we value opensource technology, borderless finance, financial curiosity, choice & freedom. As we look out between the years of 2020 – 2040, SoFL Excellence Academy has the following core beliefs:

- It is not too late to join the digital asset revolution
- A new class of wealth will be created due to Bitcoin and digital finance
- Currently as every company is a technology company because of the internet, by 2040, every company will be a digital asset company because of Bitcoin and blockchain

- There is a fifty percent chance that a digital asset will become the global reserve currency.
- Institutional and consumer mass adoption of Bitcoin and digital assets is a bit away, but Bitcoin and digital assets will eventually become mainstream and the world will seamlessly interact with this new asset class solely or side by side with the existing traditional financial markets.

The origin of this company started when my wife and I were planning our relocation to the South Florida area from Cleveland, Ohio. We had been putting the pieces together to move our family for over twelve months. Then COVID-19 hit. This slowed our physical move, but it did not stop our drive to accomplish our goals. In fact, the pandemic acted as a catalyst to motivate us to introduce Excellence to the world.

Our premier product and service is our **#RabbitHoleResouce** – Educational Training Workshop – SoFL Excellence Academy, aptly named after our company. This training workshop is an annual, exclusive, onsite training academy that focuses on introducing digital and decentralized business, finance, and technology to a select group of young women and minority students enrolled in high school STEM programs throughout the United States.

The SoFL Excellence Academy offers an annual two-and-a-half-day training curriculum, set over the third weekend in June (Fri, Sat, 1/2-day Sun), on a participating local college or business campus, in Miami, Florida. The first workshop is set to open in June of 2021. This exclusive academy is available and free to students sixteen years old and older, who only need to apply for admission to one of the competitive 300 available spots. The awarded students receive a grant scholarship to cover their three-day training program, thanks to our various donors, corporate partners, and sponsors.

The goal of the SoFL Excellence Academy training workshop is to foster mass adoption of Bitcoin and digital currencies among the brightest young adults and to create digital finance early adopters from the historically underrepresented minorities and women, who have been traditionally left out or lag in business, finance and technology innovations. Although we believe that STEM programs have been instrumental in creating inclusion for women and minority groups in the US economy, we believe that the knowledge of digital finance is currently missing in most high school curriculum but needed for young adults to eventually compete in the new global digital economy. Therefore, the SoFL Excellence Academy targets those STEM students who already understand the importance of higher learning and introduces the students to current industry and thought leaders in the field of global finance, who will facilitate workshops demonstrating how digital money moves globally now and, in the future, and prepares the students for inclusion into the new global finance economy without borders.

The students will learn everything they need to know about Bitcoin and decentralized finance as a technology protocol, a currency, and a store of value, and how global businesses, governments, and central banks are beginning to adopt blockchain and crypto technology to create their own digital asset use cases. In the workshop, students will get firsthand experience creating their own digital wallet and digital asset. Students can use the knowledge and resources gained from this academy as a fundamental foundation to guide their education, career, and financial aspirations into the future.

In addition to the Educational Training Workshop, SoFL Excellence Academy will produce a free weekly podcast #**RabbitHoleResouce** – called *The Excellence Podcast*. Each week we will reach thousands of young minorities and women, STEM students, aspiring technology entrepreneurs, rising investment professionals, and diversity and inclusion professionals, with our free content to better understand how business, finance and technology CEOs and founders intersect with the Bitcoin and digital asset industry. We will provide analysis of recent news, industry trends, summaries of private conversations with industry insiders, rising digital asset companies, and other areas of interest for the financial and technology curious of all types. Whether you are a crypto O.G or you are brand new to the digital business space, this information will better prepare you for participating in the ever-changing world of digital business, finance, and technology.

The third product and service of SoFL Excellence Academy is our first product to launch, the best-selling book that you are reading now, **#RabbitHoleResouce** – *Deep into the Bitcoin Rabbit Hole – Take a Journey into the World of Crypto and Discover the 3 Keys to Unlock Your Financial Destiny,* and our free companion guide, *Rabbit Hole Resource Guide.* This is the first book and companion guide in a series of planned books to be published periodically corresponding with significant Bitcoin events such as the Bitcoin Halving. For example, in 2024 look out for a following book titled *"Block 840,000 – Bitcoin Halving Number 4".*

SoFL Excellence Academy has come into the world right at the time when the United States is finally trying to reckon with the structural and institutional racism that has plagued the United States of America for the last 400 years. We at SoFL Excellence Academy offer our expertise in diversity, equity, and inclusion education to our clients and it could not come at a better time. Individuals, companies, and organizations all over the nation are now grappling with social justice and equity issues because of the recent murders of George Floyd and other Black men and women at the hand of US law enforcement.

Following the killing of George Floyd, groups such as **#BlackExcellence** – Black Lives Matter, organized daily protest around the country. Some of the world's most influential organizations have donated large sums of money to campaigns against racial injustice, and thousands of people of all races have marched in solidarity. Some encouraging first steps have been announced by the public sector to address the issue of systemic racism.

At SoFL Excellence Academy, we agree with the crypto community that Bitcoin is a peaceful protest option. We teach that the Bitcoin network is a way for marginalized people to opt out of the traditional financial system that has been historically plagued with systemic and institutionalized racism. There is racism within the Bitcoin community, however, as the Bitcoin protocol is a software program, Bitcoin itself is not inherently racist.

Fortunately, we are starting to see a zero-tolerance approach to racial injustice sweeping across the corporate world in the United

States. Companies are beginning to implement a rash of progressive corporate policies on diversity, equity, and inclusion. At SoFL Excellence Academy, diversity, equity, and inclusion is a cornerstone of our busines. We believe that Bitcoin can serve as your affirmative action plan.

However, it is now time to see if other companies, governments, and societies can follow up their policies and procedures with the real structural reforms needed to create better opportunities for Black people and underrepresented populations everywhere.

I do not think it will be easy, but at SoFL Excellence Academy, we have some good ideas on how to go about it. It all begins with education and acknowledgment of the problem. We have seen that many other companies have pledged their support for Black Lives Matter and other campaigns against racial injustice. Also there has been pressure on companies everywhere for real-life, measurable support. Nike has publicly pledged $40 million over four years to support Black community initiatives, as well as stepping up measures to attract a more diverse workforce. And there have been other large donations from Silicon Valley giants, including Amazon, Airbnb, Uber, YouTube, and Facebook. (61)

Beyond the world of business, we at SoFL Excellence Academy believes that simple public crowdfunding can help people target their donations with precision. SoFL Excellence Academy is a company whose mission is to support efforts in financial diversity, equity, and inclusion. We rely on donations from our corporate partners and sponsors to fund our Academy and podcast, which provides education and access to tools that can fight social and economic injustice. We accept bitcoin donations directly from the public. If any of our readers are so inclined to donate bitcoin to our work in these areas, we very much appreciate it and provide you with the following Bitcoin Donation Address where you can make your contribution:

3LVUBrjqXmMxroFvCE5bNdBswYPhr4ts22

When it comes to bitcoin, SoFL Excellence Academy is a bitcoin first company. This means that any product and service that we offer, we will accept bitcoin and other traditional forms of US dollar payments. However, if you choose to interact with us in bitcoin, you will always receive at minimum, a twenty percent discount to the regular US dollar price. We offer this incentive on our book and Academy content, to encourage our clients to begin to participate in the digital asset economy on the way to mass adoption.

However, donations can only go so far, and businesses are under pressure to turn financial goodwill into tangible solutions. Some of these solution ideas can be relatively simple. For example, Twitter co-founder and CEO Jack Dorsey made Juneteenth a company holiday for Twitter and Square. June 19th commemorates the end of slavery in the United States.

(62)

Jack leading the way again. However, deeper reforms are also needed, particularly to workforce structure and pay.

According to a 2016 Federal Reserve Board survey, the median white family had more than ten times the wealth of the median Black family in 2016. This illustrates the deep and pronounced wealth gap between Black and white families, one that has been getting worse over time. Fighting this wealth gap with the early adoption of bitcoin is one of the solutions that we offer as a solution to fight this systemic issue.

Of course, there are several other ways that individuals, the government, and corporate America are trying to propose to resolve this problem. My favorite of all the ideas is paying Blacks reparations. #BlackExcellence – Robert Johnson, original founder of BET, has recently proposed $14 trillion in compensation for slavery as a way of closing the wealth gap. I believe his plan called for a payment of approximately $331,000 for each African American in the Unites States. Just like Russel Okung, all I have to say is, "Pay me in bitcoin"!

In an article published on July 13, 2020 we learned that a movement by the nation's mayors, backed a national call for reparations for the forty-one million black people in the US. The price tag on their program is about $6.2 quadrillion. This would represent a payment of $151 million to each of the forty-one million African American in the United States. Pay me in bitcoin! The US Conference of Mayors released a letter backing a Democratic plan to form a reparations commission to come up with a payment for slavery. The letter stated in part,

> "We recognize and support your legislation as a concrete first step in our larger reckoning as a nation, and a next step to guide the actions of both federal and local leaders who have promised to do better by our black residents," (63)

#BlackExcellence – Senator Cory Booker and Representative Sheila Jackson Lee have introduced legislation to create a commission, the Commission to Study and Develop Reparation Proposals for African Americans Act.

I am hopeful but certain that the US government is not going to pay Black people reparations within my lifetime. Although we know that they can turn on the printing press of the US dollar any time they choose. We have seen the printer go Brrrr to the tune of $5 trillion just in the last couple of months. Whether they pay or not, bitcoin fixes this and SoFL Excellence Academy is here to facilitate everyone's knowledge of digital assets. If the US government does pay trillions or quadrillions to settle the reparations, future generations will need a sound money currency like bitcoin to protect their wealth from the impending hyperinflation of the US dollar to come. If the US government does not pay up, Black people can just opt out of the traditional financial system and have bitcoin serve as their Bitcoin Reparations. Either way, SoFL Excellence Academy will be here to serve the needs of the community

To close out this chapter and book, I would be remiss if I did not recognize and thank my wife for supporting my twenty-six-month journey deep into the Bitcoin rabbit hole. Without her support, my journey would have been cut short. She was the driving force behind establishing the SoFL Excellence Academy and her encouragement and support is responsible for this completed book and turning me into a first-time author. She is my inspiration and I hope that she can be an inspiration to others.

In honor of her Bitcoin journey, we at SoFL Excellence Academy carry as one of our branding taglines, the hashtag **#BlackWomenInBitcoin**. We want to see this hashtag go viral as we strive to make the bitcoin community more diverse and inclusive.

To obtain more information on SoFL Excellence Academy, visit our website at:

http://www.SoFLExcellenceAcademy.com

or email us at:

info@SoFLExcellenceAcademy.com

The End.

WORKS CITED

1. **Tradingview.** Bitcoin USD (BTC-USD). *tradingview.com.* [Online] August 16, 2020. https://www.tradingview.com/symbols/BTCUSD/.

2. **Roberts, Daniel.** IRS adds specific crypto question to 2019 tax form. *Finance.Yahoo.com.* [Online] January 7, 2020. https://finance. yahoo.com/news/irs-adds-specific-crypto-question-to-2019-tax-form-192521373.html.

3. **Office of the Comptroller of the Currency.** Brian P. Brooks Named OCC Chief Operating Officer. *OCC.gov.* [Online] March 16, 2020. https://www.occ.gov/news-issuances/news-releases/2020/ nr-occ-2020-33.html#:~:text=WASHINGTON%E2%80%94The%20 Office%20of%20the,%2C%20effective%20April%201%2C%202020..

4. —. Federally Chartered Banks and Thrifts May Provide Custody Services For Crypto Assets. *OCC.gov.* [Online] July 22, 2020. https:// www.occ.gov/news-issuances/news-releases/2020/nr-occ-2020-98. html.

5. **Bitcoins Channel.** US Gallup Poll Shows Only 2% of American Investors Own Bitcoin. *bitcoinschannel.com.* [Online] July 27, 2018. https://bitcoinschannel.com/us-gallup-poll-shows-only-2-of-amer-ican-investors-own-bitcoin/.

6. **99Bitcoins.com.** It has no intrinsic value. [Online] [Cited: May 13, 2020.] https://99bitcoins.com/bitcoin-obituaries/.

7. **Lee, Timothy B.** The $11 million in bitcoins the Winklevoss brothers bought is now worth $32 million. *washingtonpost.com.* [Online] November 9, 2013. https://www.washingtonpost.com/ news/the-switch/wp/2013/11/09/the-11-million-in-bitcoins-the-winklevoss-brothers-bought-is-now-worth-32-million/.

8. **Antonopoulos, Andreas M.** BTC2019: Certified Bitcoin Profes-sional (CBP) Prep Course. Seattle : s.n., August 28, 2019.

9. **Merriam-Webster.** Bitcoin. [Online] July 27, 2020. https://www. merriam-webster.com/dictionary/Bitcoin.

10. **Khatri, Yogita.** Two firms merge to open 100-acre bitcoin mining

farm in Texas, with a capacity of one gigawatt. *TheBlockCrypto.com.* [Online] November 20, 2019. https://www.theblockcrypto.com/ post/47717/two-firms-merge-to-open-100-acre-bitcoin-mining-farm-in-texas-with-a-capacity-of-one-gigawatt.

11. **Tiwari, Teeka.** The Second Boom: How to Make a Fortune From the Next Crypto Run Up. [Online] 2018. [Cited: April 15, 2018.]

12. **Woo, Wilma.** Top 10 Expert Bitcoin Price Preditions for 2018 & Beyond. [Online] April 16, 2018. https://bitcoinist.com/10-bitcoin-price-predictions-2018-beyond/.

13. **Dorsey, Jack.** Twitter. [Online] March 20, 2019. https://twitter.com/Jack.

14. **Binance Academy.** Binance Academy Glossary. [Online] [Cited: June 12, 2020.] https://academy.binance.com/glossary.

15. **Helms, Kevin.** Akon City: $6 Billion Cryptocurrency City Set to Begin Cnstruction. *Bitcoin.com.* [Online] June 20, 2020. https://news.bitcoin.com/akon-city-akoin-cryptocurrency/.

16. **POLLOCK, DARRYN.** The Cream of the Crypto Crop: 10 Best Performing Assets in 2017. *Cointelegraph.com.* [Online] January 3, 2018. https://cointelegraph.com/news/the-cream-of-the-crypto-crop-10-best-performing-assets-in-2017.

17. **Blockland Solutions Conference.** Blockland Solutions. [Online] December 3, 2018. https://www.blocklandsolutions.com/.

18. **Bamforth, Emily.** Blockland Solutions Conference is Over: What's Next for Blockchain in Cleveland? *Cleveland.com.* [Online] December 4, 2018. https://www.cleveland.com/news/2018/12/ blockland-solutions-conference-is-over-whats-next-for-block-chain-in-cleveland.html.

19. **Fortune.** JP Morgan Files Patent for Blockchain-Powered Payments. [Online] [Cited: August 24, 2018.]

20. **RTTTNews.** Capital One Files Patent For Blockchain-based User Authentication. [Online] [Cited: August 24, 2018.]

21. **American Banker.** Banks pour $107M into blockchain consor-

tium R3. [Online] [Cited: August 24, 2018.]

22. **Cointelegraph.** CEO of UBS: Blockchain Will Transform Cost Base of Financial Services Industry. [Online] [Cited: August 24, 2018.]

23. **Fortune.** Here's Why Bank of America Has Filed Nearly 50 Blockchain-Related Patents. [Online] [Cited: August 24, 2018.]

24. —. Banking Giants Including Citigroup and Barclays Sign Up for a Trial Blockchain Project. [Online] [Cited: August 24, 2018.]

25. **Bloomberg.** Morgan Stanley Joins Goldman Sachs in Clearing Bitcoin Futures. [Online] [Cited: August 24, 2018.]

26. **Cointelegraph.** Morgan Stanley Hires Credit Suisse Crypto Expert as Head of Digital Asset Markets. [Online] [Cited: August 24, 2018.]

27. **Wikipedia.** Michael Novogratz. [Online] [Cited: May 30, 2020.] https://en.wikipedia.org/wiki/Michael_Novogratz.

28. **Ethereal Summit.** Mike Novogratz, The Herd is coming (Ethereal, SF, 2017). *YouTube.* [Online] [Cited: June 15, 2020.] https://www.youtube.com/watch?v=9zSPKYvZth4.

29. **Dvir.** The Crypto Sphere. *listennotes.com.* [Online] https://www.listennotes.com/podcasts/the-crypto-sphere-dvir-SRKsXPVI8mW/.

30. **Loeffler, Kelly.** Introducing Bakkt. *Medium.com.* [Online] August 3, 2018. https://medium.com/bakkt-blog/introducing-bakkt-e1794dd3a45d.

31. **The Gentlemen of Crypto.** The Gentlemen of Crypto. *YouTube.com.* [Online] [Cited: September 30, 2018.] https://www.youtube.com/channel/UCJ0QV-XhATeq4-hTgqMz1TQ.

32. **Chaparro, Frank.** Fidelity Digital Assets Eyes Services for Introducing Crypto Funds to Big Investors. *theblockcrypto.com.* [Online] June 24, 2020. https://www.theblockcrypto.com/daily/68920/fidelity-digital-assets-eyes-service-for-introducing-crypto-funds-to-big-investors.

33. **TD Ameritrade.** Announcing an investment in ErisX -- a

regulated exchange for cryptocurrency. *tdameritrade.com.* [Online] [Cited: June 15, 2020.] https://www.tdameritrade.com/investment-products/cryptocurrency-trading.page.

34. **Shawdagor, Jinia.** Ivy League Universities Set to Boost the Crypto Industry with an Injection of Institutional Investment. *cointelegraph.com.* [Online] May 28, 2019. https://cointelegraph.com/news/ivy-league-universities-set-to-boost-the-crypto-industry-with-an-injection-of-institutional-investment.

35. **Pompliano, Anthony.** The Pomp Podcast. *anthonypomliano.com.* [Online] [Cited: May 20, 2020.] https://anthonypompliano.com/.

36. **Wikipedia.** Lindy Effect. [Online] [Cited: June 24, 2020.] https://en.wikipedia.org/wiki/Lindy_effect.

37. **Constine, Josh.** Facebook Announces Libra Cryptocurrncy: All You Need to Know. *Techcrunch.com.* [Online] June 18, 2019. https://techcrunch.com/2019/06/18/facebook-libra/?guccounter=1&-guce_referrer=aHR0cHM6Ly93d3cuZ29vZ2xlLmNvbVS8&-guce_referrer_sig=AQAAAFkTwgKVZydhr65fHqcDH1JUD0b-plE9Z9GR2vNAwI6Rm0T7JkBnnxpoweWZLFRDhReR4DjJoD-NE39xYZ1S0cfMHXqqwFVrZSeQBJjiFzJNXpqood-23DI3D6k5RDO.

38. **Brown, Ben.** 21 Brutally Honest Opinions About Facebook's Libra Cryptocurrency. *CCN.com.* [Online] June 22, 2019. https://www.yahoo.com/entertainment/21-brutally-honest-opinions-facebook-164533882.html.

39. **Libra.** Libra Whitepaper. *libra.org.* [Online] [Cited: July 15, 2019.] https://libra.org/en-US/white-paper/.

40. **U.S. House Committe on Financial Service.** Committee Democrats Call on Facebook to Halt Cryptocurrenty Plans. *Financialservices.house.gov.* [Online] July 2, 2019. https://financialservices.house.gov/news/documentsingle.aspx?DocumentID=404009.

41. **Hamilton, Jesse.** Fed's Jerome Powell has 'Serious Concerns' with Facebook Libra Proposal. *Bloomberg.com.* [Online] July 10, 2019. https://www.bloomberg.com/news/articles/2019-07-10/fed-s-powell-has-serious-concerns-with-facebook-libra-proposal.

42. **Trump, Donald.** Twitter.com. [Online] July 12, 2019. https://twitter.com/realDonaldTrump.

43. **Battrick, Ray.** Federal Reserve Exploring Central Bank Digital currency. *Businessblockchainhq.com.* [Online] February 11, 2020. https://businessblockchainhq.com/business-blockchain-news/federal-reserve-exploring-central-bank-digital-currency/.

44. **Johnson, Brian.** The Top 3 Cashless Countries. *CoreCashless.com.* [Online] [Cited: August 2, 2020.] https://www.corecashless.com/the-worlds-top-3-cashless-countries/.

45. **Lagarde, Christine.** Twitter.com. [Online] November 14, 2019. https://twitter.com/Lagarde.

46. —. LinkedIn.com. [Online] [Cited: June 1, 2020.] https://www.linkedin.com/in/christinelagarde.

47. **Investopedia.** Qantitative Easing. [Online] [Cited: June 1, 2020.] https://www.investopedia.com/terms/q/quantitative-easing.asp#:~:text=Quantitative%20easing%20(QE)%20is%20a,and%20encourage%20lending%20and%20investment..

48. **CNBC Television.** Paul Tudor Jones Calls bitcoin 'Fastest Horse' in This Environment. *YouTube.com.* [Online] May 7, 2020. https://www.cnbc.com/video/2020/05/07/paul-tudor-jones-calls-bitcoin-fastest-horse-in-this-environment.html.

49. **Okung, Russell.** Twitter.com. [Online] May 13, 2019. https://twitter.com/RussellOkung.

50. **Staff, Daily Hodl.** Chargers' Russell Okung Says Bitcoin Is Freedom After Bank Denies Request to Withdraw His Own Money. *dailyhodl.com.* [Online] October 14, 2019. https://dailyhodl.com/2019/10/14/chargers-russell-okung-says-bitcoin-is-freedom-after-bank-denies-request-to-withdraw-his-own-money/.

51. **Rolling, J. K.** Twitter.com. [Online] May 15, 2020. https://twitter.com/jk_rowling.

52. **McCormark, Peter.** The Beginner's Guide To Bitcoin. *Whatditcoindid.com.* [Online] January 15, 2020. https://www.whatbitcoindid.com/the-beginners-guide-to-bitcoin.

53. **Kiyosaki, Robert.** Twitter.com. [Online] May 16, 2020. https://twitter.com/theRealKiyosaki.

54. **Amazon.** Mastering Bitcoin: Programming the Open Blockchain 2nd Edition. *Amazon.com.* [Online] [Cited: June 30, 2020.] https://www.amazon.com/Mastering-Bitcoin-Programming-Open-Blockchain-ebook/dp/B071K7FCD4.

55. **Ammous, Saifedean.** *The Bitcoin Standard.* Hoboken : John Wiley & Sons, Inc., 2018.

56. **Jackson, Isaiah.** *Bitcoin and Black America.* Los Angeles : Independently published, 2019.

57. **Twain, Mark.** Time to be in the pick and shovel business. [Quote].

58. **Crunchbase.** Discover innovative companies and the people behind them. *Crunchbase.com.* [Online] [Cited: July 31, 2020.] https://www.crunchbase.com/.

59. **Schoen, Greg.** Twitter.com. [Online] May 16, 2011. https://twitter.com/gregschoen.

60. **Brookins, Christopher.** MicroStrategy Just Sent Green Light To Corporate America On Bitcoin. *Forbes.com.* [Online] August 14, 2020. https://www.forbes.com/sites/christopherbrookins/2020/08/14/microstrategy-just-sent-green-light-to-corporate-america-on-bitcoin/#56e250426bc4.

61. **NIKE, inc.** NIKE, Inc. Statement on Commitment to the Black Community. *Nike.com.* [Online] June 5, 2020. https://news.nike.com/news/nike-commitment-to-black-community.

62. **Dorsey, Jack.** *Twitter.com.* [Online] June 9, 2020. https://twitter.com/jack.

63. **Sara Durr.** U.S. Conference of Mayors President Writes to Senator Booker, Rep. Jackson Lee to Express Support for Their Legislation on Reperations. *usmayors.org.* [Online] July 13, 2020.

64. **Wikipedia.** Bitcoin. [Online] [Cited: May 20, 2020.]

ABOUT THE AUTHOR

Damon L Johnson is a financial Services professional, entrepreneur, and first-time author of the highly anticipated book, *Deep into the Bitcoin Rabbit Hole*. He has spent over twenty-five years as a technology manager in the traditional banking industry, where he developed his passion for data analytics and digital finance. His first-hand experience in the traditional banking industry has given him an up-close view of the various problematic issues within the traditional financial system.

In 2018, Damon began his journey into the alternative financial world of Bitcoin and cryptocurrencies and in 2020, his passion and entrepreneurial spirit lead him and his wife Angela, to co-found their family business, SoFL Excellence Academy – a digital finance education and training consultancy company, as a new resource for people who have been historically underrepresented and tradition-ally left behind in the traditional financial system.

Damon has a BA from The Ohio State University and an MBA from the University of Phoenix. He has been actively involved in the North East Ohio and South Florida communities as an active member of the National Black MBA Association and a proud active member of Alpha Phi Alpha Fraternity, Incorporated since 1988.

You can follow Damon's journey into the world of Bitcoin and crypto by downloading his free *Rabbit Hole Resource Guide* at

http://www.RabbitHoleResourceGuide.com.

You can also follow him on Twitter @AuthorDLJohnson

THANK YOU FOR READING MY BOOK!

I really appreciate all your feedback, and I love hearing what you have to say.

I need your input to make the next version of this book and my future books better.

Please leave me an honest review on Amazon letting me know what you thought of the book.

Thanks so much!

Damon L Johnson

Made in the USA
Monee, IL
03 October 2020